BEN FLOWERS

1000 Amazing Facts About Britain For Kids

Hope you have happy memories of the UK with this book :)

Love,

Usha patti, sruthi a gukan

This book was professionally typeset on Reedsy.
Find out more at reedsy.com

Contents

Foreword

Hello, my name is Ben. I am a dad of three girls who lives in the north-east of England. I am forever attempting to get my kids (15, 9 and 3 years old) off their devices and actually learn something. "But Dad, this YouTube short is teaching me about K-pop!" I often hear or something else of that nature. But I digress....

Anyway, I have written this fact book with the sole purpose of teaching my kids some general knowledge about Britain the wonderful place where they were born and raised.

The book is presented as a collection of facts. The idea behind this is to inspire some conversation around the topics and perhaps do some extra research on the web or some days out discovering! For those who really get into it, I have created some epic quizzes at the back to test your knowledge of all things Britain. You could use these quizzes for family quiz nights and the like.

The main thing is that you have fun reading through them, learn some stuff, and perhaps even decide you want to know more about any of the topics presented. Just imagine, stopping scrolling, putting that device down and discovering that Britain is actually, pretty cool.

Thanks so much for getting this book and hopefully you will enjoy it as much as I will ensure my kids do. Ha ha.

Thanks, Ben

I

Facts About Britain

Us British and our lands are a weird and wonderful collection of people and places. There are so many amazing facts about Britain you could read them forever... But here are a thousand to get you started!

1

Britain

Well? Where to start? It's probably best to just jump straight into some general facts about Britain to get ourselves nice and warm. Let's make a start.

- Britain or the United Kingdom (UK) comprises four countries: England, Scotland, Wales, and Northern Ireland. Scotland to the far north, Wales to the west, Northern island over the sea and England to the south.
- The capital city of England and the UK is London. It's very big and very busy!
- The British flag is called the Union Jack, and it combines the flags of England, Scotland, and Ireland. The colour is Red, White and Blue.
- The King of the United Kingdom is King Charles III. His wife is Queen Camilla.
- The famous clock tower in London is called Big Ben. It is the nickname for the Great Bell of the Clock at the north end of the Palace of Westminster.
- The River Thames flows through London, and it is the longest river entirely in England.
- Scotland is known for its beautiful Lochs (lakes), including Loch Ness, famous for the mythical creature "Nessie." Sometimes referred to as "The Lock Ness Monster."
- Wales has over 600 castles, known as the "Land of Castles."
- Northern Ireland is home to the Giant's Causeway, a natural rock forma-

tion with interlocking basalt columns.
- Stonehenge is an ancient stone circle located in England, and its purpose is still a mystery...
- The UK is known for its love of tea, and "afternoon tea" is a popular tradition with sandwiches, cakes, and of course, tea.
- The English language originated in England and is now one of the most widely spoken languages in the world.
- The UK is famous for its iconic double-decker buses and black taxis. A Double-Decker is also a nice chocolate bar!
- Cricket and football (soccer) are very popular sports in the UK.
- The King's Guard at Buckingham Palace is known for their red uniforms and tall black hats.
- The Tower of London is an ancient fortress holding Crown Jewels, including the Crown, Scepter, and Orb.
- The British Museum in London has a vast collection of artefacts from all around the world.
- The UK celebrates many colourful festivals, including Bonfire Night and the Notting Hill Carnival.
- The world's first steam locomotive, built by George Stephenson, was called "The Rocket."
- The first passenger steam train route was from Stockton-On-Tees to Darlington in the north-east of England in 1825.
- The British love their pets; the most popular pet is the dog and some people like cats. There is a saying, "You're either a dog or a cat person." I have two dogs. I have never liked cats...
- The Beatles, a famous British band, are considered one of the greatest music groups of all time.
- The UK has the oldest public zoo in the world, called London Zoo.
- The famous detective character Sherlock Holmes was created by British author Sir Arthur Conan Doyle.
- The King's official London residence is Buckingham Palace.
- The currency used in the UK is the British Pound Sterling (£).
- The British drink over 165 million cups of tea every day!

- The London Eye is a giant Ferris wheel that offers breathtaking city views.
- The UK has over 1,000 museums, including the Natural History Museum and the Science Museum.
- The first postage stamp called the Penny Black, was used in the UK in 1840.
- The English Channel separates the UK from mainland Europe.
- The Bard of Avon, William Shakespeare, is one of the most famous playwrights and poets in the world.
- The UK is known for its beautiful countryside and picturesque villages.
- The UK has the oldest underground railway system in the world, known as the London Underground or "the Tube."
- The River Severn is the longest river in the UK.
- Britain also has many smaller islands that are close to the main countries. Such as The Isle of Wight and The Isles of Scilly.
- The UK is a constitutional monarchy, which means the King is the head of state, but the country is run by elected officials.
- The UK celebrates Guy Fawkes Night on November 5th with fireworks and bonfires to remember the Gunpowder Plot (more later on this).
- The English town of Stratford-upon-Avon is the birthplace of William Shakespeare.
- The King's birthday is on the 14th of November
- The UK is home to some of the world's most famous universities, including Oxford and Cambridge.

2

Gruesome Britain

This chapter is all about some of the gory aspects of Britain's History. Kids of a nervous disposition may want to look away... But if you're curious read on.

- During the Black Death in the 14th century, people who were infected with the plague had awful black swellings on their bodies, giving the disease its name. The plague was spread around by rats.
- The Tower of London was used as a prison, and some prisoners were kept in dark and damp dungeons, that reeked with the stench of body odour and poo.
- Execution by beheading was a common punishment for treason in British history. There were a few ways to do this but the good old axe was the easiest.
- The Tudor king, Henry VIII, famously had six wives, and two of them were beheaded! What a nice guy he must have been.
- During the medieval period, public executions were a popular form of entertainment for the crowds. Almost like a medieval YouTube...
- Ancient Britons practised human sacrifice in their religious ceremonies. Praying quietly, or meditating just wasn't enough for them...
- The Romans used crucifixion as a punishment for serious crimes. Jesus Christ is a prime example of this. Nailed to a cross through the hands and feet and left there.

- The Tower of London's most famous execution site, Tower Green, witnessed the beheading of many prominent figures, including Anne Boleyn and Lady Jane Grey. I wonder if you needed to buy tickets to spectate?
- In the 17th century, people believed in witches, and many were accused of witchcraft and executed. A popular test was "Witch Swimming" This was the practice of tying up and dunking the accused into a lake to determine whether they sink or float. Sinking to the bottom indicated that the accused was innocent, but now very much dead, while floating indicated a guilty verdict. Which meant the death penalty. The logic here is flawless...
- The Vikings were known to use the "Blood Eagle" torture method, where the victim's ribs were cut and their lungs pulled out to resemble wings. How lovely and such a creative name.
- The "Iron Maiden" was a notorious torture device used in Britain during the Middle Ages. It had sharp spikes inside, and the victim was locked inside and slowly impaled. Can you think of anything worse?
- In medieval times, leeches were used as medical treatment to "drain" sickness from a person's body. Leeches are parasite worms that drink blood. Yuck.
- The plague doctors who treated victims of the Black Death wore creepy masks with long beaks filled with sweet-smelling herbs, as they believed bad smells caused the disease. These were called "Duck Masks" due to them looking like beaks.
- In the Tower of London, the Yeoman Warders, also known as Beefeaters, were once responsible for torturing prisoners. I wonder if they kept their red uniforms on to hide any stains?
- In the Middle Ages, "thumb screws" were used as a torture device to crush a person's fingers. Used as a punishment device for naughty soldiers.
- During the Tudor period, people believed that rubbing the fat of an executed criminal on their body could cure certain ailments... Probably works better than botox!
- The "Scavenger's Daughter" was a torture device used during the reign of Henry VIII to crush and contort the body of the victim. Think of wrapping elastic bands around your hand over and over until tight. Like that but

your whole body twisted in metal.

- Ancient Britons practised head hunting and displayed the severed heads of their enemies on poles with pride. Probably was a large problem with flies though.
- The Tower of London is said to be haunted, with ghost stories of former prisoners and beheaded queens.
- In the 16th and 17th centuries, criminals were sometimes publicly hung, drawn, and quartered, which involved being hanged until nearly dead, then disembowelled, and their body parts displayed around the country.
- In the 17th century, "witch pricking" involved using sharp instruments to find a "devil's mark" on a person's body, which was believed to be proof of witchcraft.
- The Vikings would sometimes drink from the skulls of their defeated enemies... Yummy.
- In medieval times, criminals could be sentenced to "pressing," where heavy stones were placed on their chests until they confessed or died.
- In the 19th century, people believed in "body snatching," where corpses were stolen and sold to medical schools for dissection.
- During the Tudor period, a "Scold's Bridle" was a metal mask with a tongue depressor that was used to punish women who were considered nagging or unruly.
- In the Middle Ages, "witch-finders" were hired to identify and prosecute people believed to be witches. A bit like the police but for witches.
- The Tower of London's ravens are said to protect the monarchy, and it's believed that if the ravens leave, the kingdom will fall!

3

British Accents and Sayings

Britain is a very complex place. Nothing is more complicated than each area's regional accents and slang words. *Let gan all awa it now mah mate. ("Lets us go all over it now my friend.")*

- The UK is home to a rich variety of regional accents, each with its own unique features and characteristics.
- The "Geordie" accent is from the Newcastle and Tyneside region. Example saying: "Howay, man, divvent be sae glum!" Which translates to "Come on, Man, Don't be so sad!"
- In Wales, there are various accents, including the "Valleys" accent and the "North Welsh" accent. Example saying: "Iechyd da!" (cheers in Welsh).
- The "Scouse" accent hails from Liverpool. Example saying: "Sound, la, going down to the chippy to get me some scran, want owt?" which translates into "Alright, mate, I'm going down to the fish and chip shop to get some food, do you want anything?"
- In Scotland, accents range from the "Glaswegian" accent to the "Highland" accent. Example saying: "Haw, mate, gonnae grab us a can o' Irn-Bru frae the shops, ya ken?" Translation "Hey, friend, will you get me a can of Irn-Bru from the store, do you know?" (Irn-Bru is a popular Scottish soft drink.).
- The "Brummie" accent comes from Birmingham. Example saying:

"Alright, bab, gonna pop to the Bull Ring for a bit of shoppin'." Which translates to "Hello, dear, I'm going to the Bull Ring shopping centre for a little bit of shopping." ("Bab" is a term of endearment often used in the West Midlands region.)

· The "Cockney" accent is associated with East London. Example saying: "Cor blimey, mate, I've only gone and found a fiver down the apples and pears!" Which Translates to "Wow, friend, I've just found five pounds on the stairs!" (In Cockney rhyming slang, "apples and pears" means "stairs," and "fiver" means five pounds.)

· In Yorkshire, the "Yorkshire" accent is known for its distinct vowel sounds. Example saying: "Ey up, lad, fancy a brew?" Which translates to "Hello, friend, would you like a cup of tea?"

· The "West Country" accent is heard in the southwest of England. Example saying: "Alright, me lover, fancy a pasty and a pint down by the sea?" Which translates to "Hello, my dear, do you want a Cornish pasty and a pint of beer by the sea?"

· In Northern Ireland, accents include the "Belfast" accent and the "Londonderry" accent. An example: "Hiya, wee man, d'ye want a wee dander doon to the chippy for a fish supper?" Translates to "Hello, young one, do you want to take a short walk down to the fish and chip shop for a fish dinner?" ("Wee" means small or little, and "dander" means a short walk.)

· The "Received Pronunciation" (RP) is considered the standard British accent often associated with the upper class. A "stage English" accent.

· The "Mancunian" accent is from Manchester. Example saying: "Hey up, our kid, going to the match at Old Trafford later, innit?" Which translates to "Hello, my sibling, I'm going to the football match at Old Trafford later, you know?" ("Our kid" is a term for a sibling, and "innit" is a colloquial contraction of "isn't it.")

· The "Norfolk" accent is from the county of Norfolk in East Anglia. An example: "Oi be orf to the coast for some fresh sea air, bor!" Translates to "I'm off to the coast for some fresh sea air, mate!" ("Orf" means "off," and "bor" is a term of endearment often used in Norfolk.)

· The "Estuary English" accent is a blend of Cockney and RP, commonly heard in the southeast.

· The "Mackem" accent is from the area around Sunderland. Example saying: "Ganna go get some git ket from tha shop." This translates to "I am going to get loads of sweets from the shop."

Here are some more random slang words used around Britain. How many do you know?

· Chuffed – Pleased or happy.
· Bloke – A man.
· Bird – A woman.
· Cheers – Thank you.
· Dodgy – Suspicious or risky.
· Knackered – Tired or exhausted.
· Bob's your uncle – Everything is all sorted.
· Blimey – An expression of surprise.
· Brolly – Umbrella.
· Gobsmacked – Astonished or speechless.
· Loo – Toilet or bathroom.
· Mate – Friend or buddy.
· Naff – Unstylish or uncool.
· Peckish – A little hungry.
· Suss – To figure something out.
· Ta – Thank you.
· Cheers – Goodbye or thanks.
· Chav – A term for a young person with a brash, uncultured style.
· Gaff – House or home.
· Telly – Television.
· Muppet – Fool or idiot.
· Muggy – Humid or unpleasantly warm.
· Numpty – A foolish or incompetent person.
· Skint – Broke or without money.
· Snog – To kiss passionately.

- Uni – University.
- Gutted – Disappointed or devastated.
- Minted – Very rich or wealthy.
- Mint – Very Good.
- Sorted – Everything is in order or arranged.
- Quid – A pound (money).
- Sarnie – Sandwich.
- Smashing – Excellent or great.
- Titchy – Very small or tiny.
- Yonks – A long time.
- Bog – Toilet.
- Chav – A term for a young person with a brash, uncultured style.
- Chuck – To throw.
- Gobby – Loud and outspoken.
- Knickers – Women's underwear.
- Off one's trolley – Crazy or insane.
- Nosh – Food or a meal.
- Snookered – In a difficult situation or unable to proceed.
- Trolleyed – Drunk or intoxicated.
- Brass monkeys – Very cold weather.
- Cob – A round bread roll.
- Gutted – Disappointed or upset.
- Hoover – To vacuum.
- Lost the plot – To become irrational or out of control.

4

British Music

We are a very musical people us Brits. We have artists from almost every genre! In this chapter, we delve into all things British music.

- The Beatles, one of the most famous British bands, were from Liverpool and are considered one of the greatest bands of all time. The Beatles were John Lennon, Paul McCartney, George Harrison and Ringo Star.
- Queen, another iconic British band, was known for their lead singer Freddie Mercury and hit songs like "Bohemian Rhapsody."
- Adele, a British singer, became a global superstar with her soulful voice and powerful ballads.
- The Spice Girls were a popular British girl group in the 1990s, known for their catchy songs and distinct personalities. There was Scary Spice, Baby Spice, Sporty Spice, Ginger Spice and Posh Spice (David Beckham's wife!)
- The bagpipes, often associated with Scotland, are a traditional musical instrument played at ceremonies all over Britain.
- The Last Night of the Proms is a famous British music event held annually in London.
- The UK has a vibrant music festival scene, including Glastonbury, Reading, and Leeds festivals.
- The Royal Albert Hall in London is a famous venue known for hosting concerts and other performances.

- The London Symphony Orchestra is one of the world's most renowned orchestras.
- The Rolling Stones, another iconic British band, is known for their rock and roll hits and has had a career spanning five decades!
- Amy Winehouse was a talented British singer known for her soulful voice and unique style.
- Elton John is a British singer-songwriter known for his flamboyant performances and hit songs like "Your Song," and "Rocket Man."
- British composer Edward Elgar's "Pomp and Circumstance March" is often played at graduation ceremonies.
- The UK has a long history of folk music, with songs passed down through generations. Most British families have at least a few folk songs they often sing while going about their day.
- The British National Anthem is called "God Save the King" (or "God Save the Queen" if the monarch is female).
- The British pop band One Direction gained fame after appearing on the TV show "The X Factor." Since then member Harry Styles has found global fame.
- The Beatles' album "Sgt. Pepper's Lonely Hearts Club Band" is considered one of the greatest albums in music history.
- London's West End is famous for its musical theatres, hosting popular shows like "The Phantom of the Opera" and "Les Misérables."
- The UK has a strong tradition of choir singing, with many famous choirs, including the King's College Choir in Cambridge.
- "Greensleeves" is a traditional English folk song believed to be written by King Henry VIII.
- The "British Invasion" in the 1960s saw several British bands, including The Beatles and The Rolling Stones, become hugely popular in the United States.
- The UK is home to famous music recording studios like Abbey Road Studios, where The Beatles recorded many of their songs.
- The hit song "Yellow Submarine" by The Beatles is about a magical submarine and is sung by the band's drummer, Ringo.

- The UK has a rich tradition of brass bands, with many small towns and villages having their own brass bands.
- The "Rule, Britannia!" song is traditionally performed at the Last Night of the Proms.
- "Swan Lake," a famous ballet, was composed by Russian composer Pyotr Ilyich Tchaikovsky but first performed in London.
- The hit song "Bohemian Rhapsody" by Queen is one of the longest songs ever to reach number one on the charts (nearly 6 minutes).
- British composer Benjamin Britten composed the children's opera "Noye's Fludde," based on the story of Noah's Ark.
- The UK has a strong tradition of street musicians and buskers performing in cities and towns. Usually with their instrument's box open for donations.
- British composer Gustav Holst's "The Planets" is a famous orchestral suite inspired by the planets in our solar system.
- The Spice Girls' hit song "Wannabe" is the best-selling single by a girl group of all time.
- "London Bridge Is Falling Down" is a popular nursery rhyme believed to date back to the 17th century.
- "Twinkle, Twinkle, Little Star" is a popular nursery rhyme that was composed by British sisters Ann and Jane Taylor.
- The British pop band Little Mix won "The X Factor" in 2011 and became one of the most successful girl groups in the UK.
- The hit song "Imagine" by John Lennon, a former member of The Beatles, is considered an anthem for peace and is famous around the world.
- "Auld Lang Syne," a traditional Scottish song, is sung on New Year's Eve in many English-speaking countries, including the US.

5

Invaders!

Throughout the history of Britain, we have had to endure a whole host of invaders from Romans to Vikings. This chapter is all about the various invasions of Britain.

- The Romans were the first to invade Britain in AD 43 and established a settlement called "Londinium", which later became London.
- The Vikings, fierce warriors from Scandinavia, raided and invaded Britain during the 8th and 9th centuries.
- The Norman Conquest occurred in 1066 when William the Conqueror, from Normandy (in present-day France), defeated King Harold II at the Battle of Hastings.
- The Spanish Armada, a fleet of Spanish ships, attempted to invade Britain in 1588, but it was defeated by the English navy.
- The Anglo-Saxons were Germanic people who settled in Britain in the early Middle Ages.
- The Celts were an ancient group of people who lived in Britain before the Roman invasion.
- The Norsemen, also known as the Northmen or Danes, were Vikings who settled in parts of Britain.
- The Scots from Scotland and the Picts, an ancient Celtic people, resisted Roman rule in the northern parts of Britain.

- The Anglo-Saxon invasion led to the establishment of the Anglo-Saxon kingdoms in various regions of Britain. These were called "Northumbria, Mercia, Wessex, Sussex, Kent, Essex and East Anglia."
- The Danelaw was a region in England where the Danish Viking laws and customs were followed.
- The Plantagenets, a royal dynasty, ruled over England from the 12th to the 15th centuries.
- The Tudors were a famous royal family in England, known for Henry VIII and Queen Elizabeth I.
- The Hundred Years' War between England and France saw several conflicts over control of parts of France.
- The Scottish Wars of Independence, led by figures like William Wallace and Robert the Bruce, aimed to free Scotland from English rule.
- The Wars of the Roses were a series of civil wars between two rival houses, the Yorks and the Lancasters, for the English throne.
- The Irish have a long history of interaction with Britain, including colonization and conflicts.
- The British Empire, at its height, ruled over territories all around the world, making it the largest empire in history.
- The Battle of Britain in World War II saw the UK successfully defend against German air attacks.
- The Normans brought feudalism to Britain, a system of government based on land ownership and loyalty.
- The Viking invasions left a lasting impact on the English language, with many Norse words being incorporated into Old English.
- The Spanish Armada's defeat in 1588 is often considered a turning point in European history.
- The Norman Conquest led to significant changes in English society and language, with French words entering the English vocabulary.
- The Tudor period was known for great cultural achievements, including the works of William Shakespeare.
- The Industrial Revolution in Britain brought about major advancements in technology and manufacturing.

- The Romans built many roads and structures in Britain that still exist today, like Hadrian's Wall.
- The Vikings were skilled shipbuilders and sailors, using their longships to travel and invade distant lands.
- The Celts were skilled metalworkers and made intricate jewellery and weapons.
- The Norse mythology of the Vikings included gods like Odin, Thor, and Loki.
- The Vikings were known for their elaborate burial practices, including ship burials.
- The Plantagenet kings, like Richard the Lionheart, were famous for their military prowess.
- The Hundred Years' War saw the emergence of legendary figures like Joan of Arc.
- The Wars of the Roses were named after the symbols of the rival houses: a white rose for York and a red rose for Lancaster.
- The British Empire played a significant role in shaping the modern world, spreading British culture and institutions to its colonies.
- The English language has borrowed words from many different languages due to the various invasions and influences throughout history.
- The Normans introduced the concept of knights and castles to England.
- The Tudor monarchs brought stability to England after years of turmoil.
- The Romans brought advanced engineering and architecture to Britain, constructing aqueducts and bathhouses.
- Throughout history, Britain has been a melting pot of different cultures and peoples, resulting in a rich and diverse heritage.

6

England

It's time to take a more detailed look at England. It isn't all Footy and roast dinners you know... There's lots of tea drinking too!

- The capital city of England is London (and also the UK), one of the largest and most famous cities in the world. I should know I have been lost in it plenty!
- The official language of England is English. However, due to massive accent variations in different regions, some people would beg to differ...
- England has a diverse climate from "rainy" in the summer to "rainy" in the winter... Wait, What? Sometimes it doesn't rain. From time to time we get some sunshine.
- England has a rich history, with evidence of human habitation dating back over 800,000 years.
- The flag of England is a red cross on a white background, known as the St. George's Cross. St. George is famous for slaying a dragon. To be fair, as you can imagine probably wasn't that easy.
- England is known for its beautiful countryside, including rolling hills, forests, and lakes. I am truly the happiest when wandering the English countryside.
- The English Channel separates England from mainland Europe. You can get a ferry from Dover to Calais in France in a few hours.

- The game of football (known as soccer in the United States) originated in England. Started by kicking a pig's bladder around. What a nice start to a sport.
- England is known for its love of tea, and "afternoon tea" is a popular tradition with sandwiches, cakes, and of course, tea. Everything Stops for tea is a very common English Mindset among most English people.
- The British royal family, including King Charles III, resides in England.
- England has a long history of famous writers, including William Shakespeare, Jane Austen, and Charles Dickens.
- The city of Manchester is known for its rich musical heritage, with bands like Joy Division, New Order and Oasis hailing from the area.
- The English invented the steam engine, revolutionizing transportation and industry.
- The English countryside is dotted with charming villages and traditional thatched-roof cottages.
- The traditional English breakfast includes bacon, eggs, sausage, beans, mushrooms, tomatoes, and toast. More often than not nowadays a sneaky American hashbrown is added.
- The Lake District in northwest England is a World Heritage Site known for its stunning lakes and mountains. You must visit the lakes at least once. It is an incredible place.
- The world's first public zoo, London Zoo, opened in England in 1828.
- England has a rich tradition of folklore, including stories of King Arthur and Robin Hood. The latter who stole from the rich to give to the poor.
- The English have a tradition of Morris dancing, a folk dance performed in elaborate costumes.
- The Oxford and Cambridge Boat Race is a famous annual rowing competition between the two universities.
- The Stone of Scone, a symbol of Scottish kingship, is kept in Westminster Abbey when not in use for coronations.
- England has a strong tradition of horse racing, with events like the Grand National and Royal Ascot.
- The London Underground, also known as "the Tube," is the oldest

underground railway system in the world.

- England is known for its unique traditional dishes, including fish and chips and roast dinners.
- The White Cliffs of Dover are famous chalk cliffs overlooking the English Channel.
- The Cotswolds, an area in southwestern England, is famous for its picturesque villages and stone cottages.
- The annual Wimbledon tennis tournament is one of the most prestigious events in the tennis calendar.
- The English have a long history of brewing beer, with many traditional pubs still serving locally brewed ales. Our local pub does a lovely assortment of IPAs.
- The English seaside has been a popular holiday destination for families for many years. Usually with beach huts on the front.
- The iconic red telephone booths and letterboxes are a familiar sight on the streets of England.
- England has a rich tradition of theatre, with the West End in London known for its world-class performances.
- The UK celebrates National Tea Day on April 21st to honour its love for tea.
- The London Marathon is one of the most popular and well-known marathons in the world.

7

British Cuisine

It's about time we have a look at the various culinary delights that Britain has to offer. If you see anything that you fancy for your lunch just jot it down and ask your parents... Jellied eels spring to mind.

- Fish and chips, deep-fried fish with potato chips, is a famous British dish loved by many. Traditionally you would have fish and chips on a Friday. This is due to religious beliefs.
- The Kings' favourite cake is said to be a fruit cake packed full of dried fruit and soaked in tea overnight.
- The Cornish pasty is a pastry filled with meat and vegetables, originally eaten by miners in Cornwall.
- The Scotch egg is a boiled egg wrapped in sausage meat and breadcrumbs, then deep-fried. It originates from Whitby in Yorkshire. Whitby is an amazing place to visit. Bram Stoker's Dracula was inspired by Whitby!
- Shepherd's pie is a classic British dish made with minced meat and mashed potatoes.
- The sticky toffee pudding is a delicious dessert made with moist sponge cake and toffee sauce. It originated from the lake district in the 1960s.
- The Bakewell tart is a sweet pastry filled with jam and almond-flavored sponge cake. It originated from Derbyshire.
- The Sunday roast is a traditional British meal featuring roast meat,

vegetables, Yorkshire pudding, and gravy.
- The Victoria sponge cake is a light and fluffy sponge filled with jam and cream.
- The full English breakfast is sometimes called a "fry-up" due to the frying of various ingredients.
- Marmite is a popular spread made from yeast extract, and people either love it or hate it! Personally, I can't get enough of the stuff and even like to mix it with hot water and drink it while watching the footy!
- HP Sauce, also known as "brown sauce," is a popular condiment enjoyed with many dishes. HP stands for Houses of Parliament from where it originated.
- Branston Pickle is a tangy vegetable relish often served with cheese sandwiches. It was once said the perfect sandwich is two slices of thick white bread with Branston pickle on either side. The cheese must be five mm thick and the sarnie cut diagonally.
- Afternoon tea was popularized in the early 19th century by Anna, the Duchess of Bedford.
- Scotch whisky is a famous alcoholic beverage from the UK
- The "Ploughman's Lunch" is a simple meal consisting of bread, cheese, and pickles.
- The UK is known for its tasty desserts, including trifle, Eton mess, and spotted dick.
- The sandwich was invented by John Montagu, the 4th Earl of Sandwich, who wanted a convenient meal while gambling.
- The "Ulster fry" is a Northern Irish variation of the full English breakfast, featuring soda bread and potato bread.
- Haggis is a traditional Scottish dish made from sheep's offal mixed with oats and spices. You can get Haggis and Chips and it is delicious!
- Bangers and Mash is a classic British dish of sausages served with mashed potatoes and gravy.
- The "Ploughman's Lunch" got its name from the traditional lunch that farmers would eat while working in the fields.
- The UK is known for its love of Indian cuisine, with chicken tikka masala

being a famous British-Indian dish. I would say that nine out of ten times this is my go-to curry.

- The "full breakfast" was traditionally served to give energy to labourers working long hours.
- The Scotch whisky is made from malted barley and aged for a minimum of three years in oak barrels.
- The Scottish shortbread is a delicious buttery cookie traditionally served on special occasions.
- Welsh cakes are a traditional treat made from a sweet, spiced dough cooked on a griddle.
- "Bubble and Squeak" is a dish made from leftover vegetables, usually from the Sunday roast, fried with potatoes and lashings of extra gravy.
- The jellied eels are a traditional East London dish, served cold with vinegar.
- The Eton mess is a dessert made with crushed meringue, strawberries, and whipped cream.
- Scottish porridge is a traditional breakfast made from oats cooked in water or milk.
- The Isle of Man is known for its tasty "Manx kippers," which are smoked herring.
- The UK has a wide variety of cheeses, including cheddar, Stilton, and Wensleydale.
- "Toad in the hole" is a dish made by cooking sausages in a batter, creating little "toads" peeking out.
- The UK has a thriving culinary scene, with many top-rated restaurants and talented chefs. Gordon Ramsay is a Scottish chef who has become world-famous and is considered one of the best chefs in the world.
- The Scottish dessert "Cranachan" is made with oats, cream, raspberries, and honey, creating a delightful combination of flavours.

8

British Literature

There are many things that are associated with us Brits and I would hope the contribution to the literary world would be one of the top.

- One of the oldest surviving works of British literature is "Beowulf," an epic poem composed in Old English.
- William Shakespeare, often regarded as the greatest playwright and poet in the English language, wrote 37 plays and 154 sonnets.
- "Pride and Prejudice" by Jane Austen is considered one of the most beloved and enduring novels in English literature.
- J.K. Rowling's "Harry Potter" series became a global phenomenon, captivating readers of all ages.
- The Brontë sisters, Charlotte, Emily, and Anne, were all famous novelists who wrote classics like "Jane Eyre" and "Wuthering Heights."
- "Alice's Adventures in Wonderland" by Lewis Carroll is a timeless children's classic, known for its whimsical and fantastical elements.
- The works of Charles Dickens, including "Oliver Twist" and "A Christmas Carol," vividly portrayed life in Victorian England.
- "The Lord of the Rings" trilogy by J.R.R. Tolkien is a cornerstone of fantasy literature and inspired a massive fan base.
- George Orwell's "1984" and "Animal Farm" are iconic dystopian novels that remain relevant to this day.

- Agatha Christie, known as the "Queen of Mystery," wrote numerous detective novels, with her character Hercule Poirot becoming famous worldwide.
- "Dracula" by Bram Stoker is a seminal Gothic novel that introduced the character of Count Dracula to popular culture.
- Mary Shelley's "Frankenstein" is often considered one of the first science fiction novels.
- "Gulliver's Travels" by Jonathan Swift is a satirical novel that follows the fantastical adventures of Lemuel Gulliver.
- Beatrix Potter's "The Tale of Peter Rabbit" revolutionized children's literature with its charming illustrations and engaging storytelling.
- The works of Sir Arthur Conan Doyle featuring Sherlock Holmes laid the foundation for modern detective fiction.
- The Romantic poets, including William Wordsworth and Lord Byron, were known for their exploration of nature, emotion, and individualism.
- Roald Dahl, a beloved children's author, wrote classics like "Charlie and the Chocolate Factory" and "Matilda."
- "Paradise Lost" by John Milton is an epic poem that retells the biblical story of the Fall of Man.
- Virginia Woolf was a prominent modernist writer known for works like "Mrs. Dalloway" and "To the Lighthouse."
- Rudyard Kipling's "The Jungle Book" introduced readers to the story of Mowgli and his animal friends.
- "The Chronicles of Narnia" series by C.S. Lewis is a beloved fantasy series loved by generations.
- The Victorian era saw the rise of serialized novels, with authors like Charles Dickens publishing their works in instalments.
- "The Canterbury Tales" by Geoffrey Chaucer is a collection of stories told by pilgrims traveling to Canterbury Cathedral.
- "Sense and Sensibility" by Jane Austen was her first published novel and set the tone for her future works.
- The Nobel Prize in Literature has been awarded to several British authors, including Rudyard Kipling, George Bernard Shaw, and Doris Lessing.

- Salman Rushdie's "Midnight's Children" won the Booker Prize in 1981 and was awarded the "Booker of Bookers" prize in 1993.
- "1984" by George Orwell introduced concepts like Big Brother and Newspeak, which have become part of the modern lexicon.
- "The Picture of Dorian Gray" by Oscar Wilde is a Gothic novel that explores themes of vanity and morality.
- "Winnie-the-Pooh" by A.A. Milne features beloved characters like Winnie-the-Pooh, Piglet, and Tigger.
- Sir Walter Scott is considered one of the pioneers of historical fiction, with works like "Ivanhoe" and "Rob Roy."
- "Treasure Island" by Robert Louis Stevenson is a classic adventure novel filled with pirates and hidden treasure.
- "Great Expectations" by Charles Dickens follows the journey of Pip, an orphan who dreams of becoming a gentleman.
- The Brontë sisters initially published their works under male pseudonyms to avoid gender bias.
- "Wuthering Heights" by Emily Brontë is a dark and passionate Gothic novel set on the Yorkshire moors.
- "The Waste Land" by T.S. Eliot is a groundbreaking modernist poem that reflects the disillusionment of the post-World War I era.
- The Booker Prize is one of the most prestigious literary awards, recognizing exceptional works of fiction.
- "The Wind in the Willows" by Kenneth Grahame follows the adventures of animals like Mole, Rat, and Toad.

9

Scotland

We focus now on the land of Haggis, Kilts and Bagpipes. The most beautiful landscapes and lashings of Iron Brew.

- Scotland is a country located in the northern part of the United Kingdom.
- The capital city of Scotland is Edinburgh.
- Scotland has its own unique culture, traditions, and even its own Gaelic language.
- The official animal of Scotland is the unicorn, which appears on the Royal Coat of Arms. I can't confirm how many unicorns there are running about in Scotland, but I can imagine a lot.
- Scotland is famous for its stunning landscapes, including mountains, lochs (lakes), and beautiful coastlines.
- The kilt is a traditional Scottish garment worn by men and is often associated with Scotland's national dress. Yes, confirmed there is no underwear worn traditionally with a kilt. Can sometimes get chilly.
- The bagpipes are a traditional Scottish musical instrument, and their distinctive sound is often heard at Scottish events and celebrations.
- Tartan is a patterned fabric with different coloured stripes, and each Scottish clan has its unique tartan design.
- The Highlands and the Lowlands are two main geographical regions in Scotland, each with its own characteristics.

- Scottish people celebrate St. Andrew's Day on November 30th, honouring their patron saint, Saint Andrew.
- The Scottish flag, known as the Saltire or St. Andrew's Cross, features a white diagonal cross on a blue background.
- Haggis is a traditional Scottish dish made from sheep's offal mixed with oats and spices, usually served with "neeps and tatties" (turnips and potatoes).
- Edinburgh Castle is a famous historical landmark in Scotland and is perched on an extinct volcano.
- Scotland has its own legendary creature called the "Kelpie," which is said to be a water horse that lures people into the water.
- The Shetland Pony is a small and sturdy breed of pony native to the Shetland Islands, a part of Scotland.
- The Highland Games are a series of traditional Scottish athletic competitions that include events like caber tossing and hammer throwing. Recently, the event has become massive.
- Scottish inventors have made significant contributions, including the telephone (by Alexander Graham Bell) and penicillin (by Alexander Fleming).
- Robert Burns, also known as Scotland's National Bard, wrote famous poems and songs, including "Auld Lang Syne."
- The Forth Bridge, a famous railway bridge in Scotland, is considered a marvel of engineering and a World Heritage Site.
- The town of St. Andrews in Scotland is known as the "Home of Golf," and it's famous for its historic golf courses.
- Scotland is renowned for its woollen textiles, including cosy tartan scarves and kilts.
- The "Highland Cow" or "Hairy Coo" is a unique breed of cattle with long, shaggy hair and distinctive curved horns.
- The Isle of Skye, located off the west coast of Scotland, is known for its rugged landscapes and dramatic scenery. It could be a location in a fantasy movie!
- Scottish Gaelic is a Celtic language spoken by some communities in

Scotland.
- Scotland has many ancient castles, including Eilean Donan Castle and Urquhart Castle, which are popular tourist attractions.
- The Outer Hebrides, a group of islands off the northwest coast of Scotland, is known for its beautiful beaches and ancient history.
- The national flower of Scotland is the thistle, a prickly purple plant that has become a symbol of the country.
- Edinburgh's annual arts festival, known as the Edinburgh Festival Fringe, is the largest arts festival in the world.
- The Isle of Lewis, part of the Outer Hebrides, is home to the famous Lewis Chessmen, a set of medieval chess pieces.
- The Scottish wildcat is a rare and elusive species of wildcat found in the Scottish Highlands.
- The town of Gretna Green in Scotland is famous for its romantic wedding traditions and elopements.
- The Scottish Borders, located along the border with England, is known for its rich history of traditional textile manufacturing.
- The "Ring of Brodgar" is a Neolithic stone circle located in Orkney, Scotland, and is believed to be over 4,500 years old.
- Scotland's stunning landscapes have served as a filming location for popular movies and TV shows, including "Harry Potter" and "Outlander."
- The traditional Scottish dish "Cullen Skink" is a hearty soup made with smoked haddock, potatoes, and onions.
- The Shetland Islands are home to a breed of small ponies known for their friendly and gentle nature.
- The Isle of Arran, often referred to as "Scotland in Miniature," features a diverse landscape with mountains, beaches, and forests.
- The Edinburgh International Book Festival is the world's largest public celebration of the written word.
- The Fairy Pools, located on the Isle of Skye, are natural pools with crystal-clear blue water that attract visitors from around the world.
- The town of Braemar hosts the annual Braemar Gathering, a traditional Highland Games event attended by members of the royal family.

- Scotland has a rich history of myths and legends, including stories of brave knights, heroic warriors, and magical creatures.
- The Hebrides, a group of islands off the west coast of Scotland, have inspired many famous works of literature and poetry.
- Scotland has its own unique system of traditional music, featuring instruments like the fiddle, bagpipes, and accordion.

10

British Humour

Sarcasm? Check. Dry Wit? Check. Taking the mick out of every single aspect of yourself? Check. We are British, and we have a funny sense of humour.

- British humour is often characterized by its dry wit and clever wordplay.
- Monty Python's Flying Circus, a British comedy sketch show, is considered a comedy classic. The "Lumberjack song" is a particularly funny one.
- The "British sense of humour" is frequently associated with the ability to find humour in awkward or uncomfortable situations.
- Stand-up comedy has a long history in the UK, with many famous comedians starting their careers on the comedy club circuit.
- "Blackadder," a historical sitcom starring Rowan Atkinson, is celebrated for its clever writing and hilarious characters. It spans four main periods in Britain's history.
- British sitcoms like "Fawlty Towers," "The Office," and "Absolutely Fabulous" have become iconic in the world of comedy. Fawlty Towers and The Office are my absolute favourite TV comedy shows of all time.
- Puns and wordplay are often used to create humour in British comedy.
- The "Carry-On" film series is a collection of British comedy movies known for their innuendos and slapstick humour.
- British panel shows, like "QI" and "Have I Got News for You," feature comedians answering questions and discussing humorous topics.

- The British are known for their self-deprecating humour, poking fun at themselves and their culture.
- "The Goon Show" was a groundbreaking radio comedy show in the 1950s that influenced generations of comedians.
- British sitcoms often use absurd and exaggerated situations to create laughs. Sometimes referred to as "Farce Comedy."
- British comedy often satirizes politics and societal norms.
- The phrase "Keep calm and carry on" has become a symbol of British humour and resilience.
- The British comedy duo Laurel and Hardy were famous for their slapstick humour and physical comedy.
- British comedians like Ricky Gervais and Stephen Fry are known for their quick wit and sharp humour.
- The sitcom "Dad's Army" humorously portrayed the Home Guard during World War II. A bunch of old men doing their best in a difficult situation.
- British comedy often includes references to British culture and history.
- The sketch comedy show "The Two Ronnies" featured the comedic duo, Ronnie Barker and Ronnie Corbett.
- British humour is appreciated globally and has influenced comedy in many other countries.
- The British comedy "Black Books" follows the misadventures of a grumpy bookshop owner.
- The British political satire "Yes Minister" mocked the workings of government.
- The British love to use irony and understatement to create humour.
- The British comedy "The Mighty Boosh" is known for its surreal and fantastical humour. Noel Fielding now presents "The Great British Bake Off."
- The "British invasion" of the 1960s brought British humour to the United States and influenced American comedy.
- British comedy often pokes fun at social classes and stereotypes.
- British sitcoms like "Only Fools and Horses" and "Dad's Army" have become part of the cultural fabric of the UK.

- British stand-up comedians often tour internationally and have global fan bases.
- The comedy show "Mock the Week" humorously discusses current events and news headlines.
- The British sitcom "Absolutely Fabulous" follows the misadventures of two eccentric and fashion-obsessed women.
- British comedy often incorporates satire, parody, and absurdity.
- British comedy has a rich history in theatre, with playwrights like Oscar Wilde known for their witty and humorous plays.
- The comedy show "Whose Line Is It Anyway?" originated in the UK and features improvisational comedy.
- The phrase "A stiff upper lip" refers to the British ability to remain calm and composed in difficult situations, even humorous ones.
- The British comedian Benny Hill was known for his slapstick humour and iconic chase scenes.
- British humour often relies on cultural references and shared experiences.
- The comedy duo Wallace and Gromit, created by Nick Park, are beloved characters known for their quirky adventures.
- The British comedy "Little Britain" features sketch comedy and satirical parodies of British culture.
- The British comedian John Cleese co-founded Monty Python and starred in "Fawlty Towers." Is considered a legend in comedy around the world.
- British comedy often plays with social taboos and boundaries.
- The British comedy "The Office," created by Ricky Gervais, has inspired various international adaptations. The US Office was a huge success and helped Steve Carrell amass global fame.

11

British Traditions and Celebrations

We have some strange traditions and celebrations in Britain... But we also have some lovely ones. Below are some of the traditions and celebrations we Brits get up to on an annual basis.

- Changing of the Guard at Buckingham Palace.
- Bonfire Night (Guy Fawkes Night) with fireworks and bonfires on November 5th. Guy Fawkes tried to blow up the houses of parliament with barrels of gunpowder "The Gunpowder Plot." Now we celebrate by making a guy Fawkes doll and often burning it on a "Bondy."
- May Day celebrations with Maypole dancing and crowning of the May Queen.
- Morris Dancing is a traditional folk dance performed on special occasions.
- Wimbledon is a prestigious tennis tournament held in London.
- Christmas Pantomimes, interactive fairy tale performances during the holiday season. Often referred to as "Panto." These little plays are fun for all the family.
- Notting Hill Carnival, a colourful Caribbean-inspired street festival in London.
- Christmas Markets with festive treats, crafts, and gifts. The perfect tradition for getting excited about Christmas.
- Harvest Festival, celebrates the end of the harvest season with music and

feasts.
- St. David's Day in Wales, honouring the patron saint of Wales with daffodils and leeks.
- Burns Night in Scotland, commemorates poet Robert Burns with haggis and poetry recitals.
- Boxing Day, the day after Christmas, is often marked with shopping and sports events. My mother used to always go shopping in the boxing day sales while my dad would go to the pub to watch football. I always had a choice of where to attend. It wasn't the shopping...
- Remembrance Day, honouring fallen soldiers and veterans with poppy-wearing and ceremonies.
- Troon Welly Boot Race, a fun race in Wellington boots on the Scottish coast.
- Cheese Rolling, chasing a wheel of cheese down a hill in Gloucestershire. This is absolutely crazy. Broken bones everywhere. But Cheese pride is everything.
- Plough Monday, blessing ploughs and enjoying Morris dancing.
- Christmas Carols, singing traditional songs during the holiday season.
- Apple Wassailing, blessing apple trees for a fruitful harvest.
- Goodwood Revival, vintage car races and retro clothing in West Sussex.
- The Last Night of the Proms, a musical festival with patriotic songs and flag-waving.
- Gurning Contests, hilarious competitions of funny face-pulling. Just a totally standard British competition. Ha ha.
- Orkney Ba Game, is a unique mass football game played through the streets of Kirkwall, Orkney.
- Portrush Raft Race, homemade rafts racing in the sea off Portrush, Northern Ireland.
- Blackberrying, picking blackberries in late summer.
- Padstow Obby-Oss, a colourful May Day celebration with dancing and singing in Cornwall.
- Haxey Hood, is a game where villagers compete for a leather tube.
- Straw Bear Festival, a person dressed as a straw bear dances in Whittlesey,

Cambridgeshire.
- Pancake Races, pancake-flipping races held on Shrove Tuesday.
- The Blackening of the Bride is a playful and messy pre-wedding tradition in parts of Scotland.
- Castleton Garland Day, the Garland King parades with a flower-covered hat in Castleton.
- Tug of War, competitions held during summer fairs and festivals.
- Oak Apple Day, commemorates the restoration of the monarchy in 1660.
- Obby-Oss Day, is a vibrant May Day celebration with music and dance in Padstow.
- Dunmow Flitch Trials, lighthearted trials where couples claim a "flitch" of bacon for marital bliss.
- Trifle Eating, trifle-eating contests at village fairs and festivals.
- Potato Day celebrates potatoes with potato sack races and potato-based treats.
- Pancake Day, also known as Shrove Tuesday, with a focus on making and eating pancakes.
- The Chelsea Flower Show, is an annual flower show held in London, showcasing beautiful gardens and plants.

12

Wales

I routinely go on holiday to Wales... It's so nice.

- The capital city of Wales is Cardiff.
- The official languages of Wales are Welsh and English.
- Wales is often referred to as the "Land of Castles" because it has more castles per square mile than any other country in the world.
- Mount Snowdon is the highest mountain in Wales and England, standing at 1,085 meters (3,560 feet) above sea level.
- The flag of Wales features a red dragon on a green and white background.
- The Welsh national anthem is called "Hen Wlad Fy Nhadau," which translates to "Land of My Fathers."
- The Welsh language, also known as Cymraeg, is one of the oldest languages in Europe and is still spoken by around 20% of the population.
- Wales has a coastline that stretches for over 1,200 kilometres (750 miles).
- The country is home to three World Heritage Sites: the Castles and Town Walls of King Edward in Gwynedd, the Pontcysyllte Aqueduct and Canal, and the Blaenavon Industrial Landscape.
- Wales is famous for its lush green landscapes, rolling hills, and beautiful valleys.
- The Brecon Beacons National Park and Snowdonia National Park are

popular destinations for outdoor enthusiasts and nature lovers.

- Wales has a strong tradition of storytelling and folklore, with myths and legends woven into its cultural fabric.
- The traditional Welsh costume includes a tall black hat, a long skirt, and a shawl.
- Rugby is a hugely popular sport in Wales, and the national team is known as the Welsh Dragons.
- The world's first national governing body for sport, the Football Association of Wales, was founded in 1876.
- The name "Wales" comes from the Old English word "Wealas," which means "foreigners" or "strangers," referring to the Celtic-speaking tribes.
- The Welsh dragon is one of the oldest national symbols in the world, dating back to the early fifth century.
- Wales has a rich musical heritage, and traditional Welsh male voice choirs are famous worldwide.
- St. David is the patron saint of Wales, and St. David's Day is celebrated on March 1st each year.
- The Eisteddfod is a traditional Welsh festival of music, poetry, and literature, held annually in various locations.
- Welsh miners used to take canaries down the mines with them to detect the presence of poisonous gases.
- The Welsh town of Llanfairpwllgwyngyllgogerychwyrndrobwllllantysilio gogogoch has one of the longest place names in the world.
- Wales has a strong tradition of male voice choirs, with some choirs dating back over a century.
- The famous Welsh poet Dylan Thomas wrote the play "Under Milk Wood" and the poem "Do Not Go Gentle into That Good Night."
- The Welsh love spoons are traditional wooden spoons carved with symbols of love and affection, often given as gifts.
- Wales has a vibrant arts scene, with many artists, musicians, and writers calling the country home.
- The Welsh mining industry played a significant role in the country's

history and economy.

- Wales is home to some unique wildlife, including the red kite and the mountain hare.
- Cardiff Castle, Caernarfon Castle, and Conwy Castle are among the most well-preserved and impressive castles in Wales.
- Wales has a rich tradition of traditional folk dancing, including clog dancing and the Welsh Morris dance.
- The Welsh national dish is cawl, a hearty soup made with meat and vegetables.
- The Welsh people are known for their warm hospitality and friendly nature.
- The largest town in Wales is Swansea, located on the south coast.
- Wales has a strong literary tradition, with many famous authors and poets hailing from the country.
- The patron saint of love, St. Dwynwen, is celebrated in Wales on January 25th.
- The Welsh have their own version of a Halloween-like celebration called "Noson Galan Gaeaf" (Calan Gaeaf Eve).
- The Welsh flag is one of the few in the world that features a mythical creature. But I know Dragons are real so ignore this fact kids.
- Wales has over 600 castles and castle ruins, showcasing its medieval history.
- The Welsh town of Hay-on-Wye is famous for its numerous bookshops and is known as the "Town of Books."
- Wales is known for its warm and wet climate, contributing to its lush and green landscapes.
- The official flower of Wales is the daffodil, which blooms in abundance in the spring.
- The oldest tree in Wales, the Llangernyw Yew, is estimated to be over 5,000 years old.
- Wales has a strong folk music tradition, with traditional instruments like the harp and fiddle being popular.
- The country's national symbol, the leek, is associated with St. David's Day

and is worn by many on this occasion.

13

Famous British Landmarks

For such a little set of islands, Britain has plenty of famous landmarks. You should make it your mission to visit all of them. Ask your parents to take you to them all during the summer holidays. Is anyone for a road trip?

- Tower Bridge, London: The drawbridge can be raised to allow tall ships to pass through the River Thames.
- Buckingham Palace, London: The official residence of the British monarch is known for its changing of the guard ceremony.
- Edinburgh Castle, Scotland: The castle sits atop an extinct volcano, offering breathtaking views of the city.
- Windsor Castle, Berkshire: It's the oldest and largest inhabited castle in the world, still used by the British royal family.
- The White Cliffs of Dover, Kent: The striking white cliffs stand as an iconic symbol of Britain's coastline.
- The Shard, London: The tallest building in the UK offers panoramic views of the city from its observation deck.
- St. Paul's Cathedral, London: The cathedral's famous dome is one of the largest in the world and was designed by Sir Christopher Wren.
- The Roman Baths, Bath: These ancient baths were used by the Romans over 2,000 years ago.

- The Giant's Causeway, Northern Ireland: This unique geological formation consists of thousands of basalt columns.
- The London Eye: The giant Ferris wheel provides stunning views of London's skyline.
- Hadrian's Wall, Northern England: Built by the Romans to defend against northern tribes, it's now a World Heritage Site.
- The Tower of London: The historic castle served as a royal palace, prison, and treasury throughout history.
- The British Museum, London: It houses an extensive collection of art and artefacts from around the world.
- The Eden Project, Cornwall: This ecological park features giant biomes containing diverse plant species from various climates.
- The Clifton Suspension Bridge, Bristol: Designed by Isambard Kingdom Brunel, the bridge spans the Avon Gorge.
- The Royal Albert Hall, London: The iconic venue hosts various concerts, events, and the Proms music festival.
- The Houses of Parliament, London: The Palace of Westminster is where the UK Parliament convenes.
- The Victoria and Albert Museum, London: Known as the V&A, it's the world's largest museum of decorative arts and design.
- The Royal Observatory, Greenwich: The Prime Meridian, marking 0 degrees longitude, runs through the observatory.
- The Natural History Museum, London: The museum's dinosaur exhibit includes a replica of a Diplodocus skeleton named "Dippy."
- Trafalgar Square, London: The square is famous for its Nelson's Column, guarded by four lion statues.
- The York Minster, York: This stunning Gothic cathedral has the largest medieval stained glass windows in the world.
- The Millennium Bridge, London: The pedestrian bridge wobbles slightly when crowded, earning it the nickname "The Wobbly Bridge."
- The Royal Pavilion, Brighton: The extravagant former royal residence was built in the Indian-style Regency architecture.
- The Millennium Dome (The O2), London: Originally built for the year

2000 celebrations, it's now a major entertainment venue.
- The Blackpool Tower, Lancashire: Inspired by the Eiffel Tower, it offers a circus, ballroom, and observation deck.
- The Lake District National Park, Cumbria: It is the largest national park in England, renowned for its stunning landscapes.
- The Angel of the North, Gateshead: This massive sculpture has a wingspan equal to that of a jumbo jet.
- The Balmoral Hotel, Edinburgh: The clock tower is intentionally set a few minutes fast to help travellers catch trains.
- St. Michael's Mount, Cornwall: This tidal island is home to a medieval castle and stunning gardens.
- The Tate Modern, London: The museum is housed in a former power station, offering modern and contemporary art.
- The Liver Building, Liverpool: The two Liver Birds on top of the building are said to protect the city.
- The Old Royal Naval College, Greenwich: The iconic buildings have been featured in many films, including "Pirates of the Caribbean."
- The Shakespeare's Globe, London: A faithful replica of the original Globe Theatre where many of Shakespeare's plays were performed.
- The Royal Yacht Britannia, Edinburgh: The former royal yacht is now a floating museum open to the public.
- The Millennium Stadium (Principality Stadium), Cardiff: The retractable roof allows games to be played in all weather conditions.
- The Science Museum, London: This interactive museum showcases scientific inventions and discoveries.
- The Royal Crescent, Bath: This grand crescent-shaped row of Georgian townhouses is a symbol of Georgian architecture.
- The Wallace Monument, Stirling: The tower commemorates Scottish hero William Wallace, the subject of the film "Braveheart."
- The National Maritime Museum, London: The museum explores the history of Britain's maritime heritage.
- The Roman Theatre of Verulamium, St. Albans: The ruins of a Roman theatre that could accommodate up to 2,000 spectators.

14

British Television

Below are some of the Greatest British TV shows of all time with some super cool facts. Many are for adults so you will have to wait until you're eighteen to watch them!

- Doctor Who: The show originally aired in 1963 and is one of the longest-running sci-fi TV series in the world. It's about a Time Lord who travels through time and space in a police public call box from the 1960s.
- Downton Abbey: The period drama series won several awards, including multiple Emmy Awards.
- Sherlock: This modern adaptation of Sherlock Holmes became an international hit and made stars out of Benedict Cumberbatch and Martin Freeman.
- Fawlty Towers: Despite having only 12 episodes, it is considered one of the greatest British sitcoms of all time. Already mentioned is one of my favs!
- The Crown: This historical drama depicts the life and reign of Queen Elizabeth II and her family.
- Monty Python's Flying Circus: The surreal sketch comedy show remains highly influential in the world of comedy starring John Cleese and Eric Idle
- Black Mirror: Known for its dark and thought-provoking themes, each

episode is a standalone story. Charlie Brooker pens all of these. They are not suitable for kids. But absolutely one for when you are eighteen years old.

- The Office (UK): Created by Ricky Gervais, this mockumentary-style sitcom became a worldwide success and was adapted in multiple countries.
- Top Gear: The motoring show gained a massive global following for its entertaining car reviews and challenges.
- EastEnders: This long-running soap opera has been on air since 1985 and continues to attract a large audience even today.
- Absolutely Fabulous: A comedy series following the outrageous antics of Edina Monsoon and Patsy Stone.
- Luther: Idris Elba's portrayal of DCI John Luther earned critical acclaim and a dedicated fan base.
- The Great British Bake Off: Known as "The Great British Baking Show" in the US, it has inspired baking enthusiasts worldwide.
- Peaky Blinders: This crime drama set in post-WWI Birmingham features the Shelby crime family.
- The X Factor UK: The reality talent show has launched numerous success-ful music careers.
- Coronation Street: The world's longest-running TV soap opera, it has been on air since 1960.
- The Graham Norton Show: The talk show features celebrity interviews and hilarious interactions with guests.
- Skins: This teen drama was praised for its realistic and unfiltered portrayal of young people.
- The IT Crowd: A comedy series revolving around the antics of employees in an IT department.
- Call the Midwife: Set in the 1950s, this drama follows midwives in London's East End.
- Gavin & Stacey: The romantic comedy series gained a cult following and returned for a one-off Christmas special in 2019.
- The Apprentice UK: Contestants compete for a chance to work with British business magnate Lord Alan Sugar.

- The Young Ones: This groundbreaking comedy series was one of the first to feature alternative comedians.
- The Inbetweeners: A comedy series following the misadventures of four friends during their school years.
- The Fall: A psychological thriller starring Gillian Anderson and Jamie Dornan.
- Line of Duty: A police procedural drama known for its intense and gripping storyline.
- The Vicar of Dibley: Dawn French stars as a female vicar in a small English village.
- Luther: The show's popularity led to the production of a feature-length film continuation of the series.
- Gavin & Stacey: The romantic comedy series gained a cult following and returned for a one-off Christmas special in 2019.
- Line of Duty: A police procedural drama known for its intense and gripping storyline.
- Father Ted: This Irish-British sitcom follows the misadventures of three priests on a remote Irish island.
- Mr. Bean: Rowan Atkinson's iconic character is known for his silent, slapstick comedy.
- Blue Planet II: This documentary series explores the wonders of the ocean and its diverse marine life.

15

UK's National Parks

The UK's National Parks a truly amazing. Below are some intriguing facts about all things UK national parks.

- There are 15 National Parks in Britain, covering about 10% of the total land area.
- The first National Park in Britain was the Peak District, established in 1951.
- The largest National Park in Britain is the Cairngorms in Scotland.
- The Lake District National Park is a World Heritage Site.
- Snowdonia National Park in Wales has the highest mountain in England and Wales, Mount Snowdon at a whooping 1085 metres high.
- The Broads, often referred to as Britain's "largest protected wetland," is a National Park in Norfolk and Suffolk and is 303 square kilometres big!
- The New Forest National Park in Hampshire is home to semi-wild ponies.
- Dartmoor National Park in Devon contains the eerie and iconic landscape of Dartmoor Prison. You can go visit it if you dare. They made it into a museum.
- The South Downs National Park is known for its stunning chalk cliffs and rolling hills.
- The Yorkshire Dales National Park is renowned for its scenic beauty and traditional stone-built villages.
- The North York Moors National Park is home to one of Britain's largest

expanses of heather moorland.
- The Pembrokeshire Coast National Park in Wales boasts breathtaking coastal scenery.
- The Brecon Beacons National Park in Wales is an International Dark Sky Reserve, making it an ideal spot for stargazing. This means no light pollution is allowed.
- The Peak District National Park contains several deep caves, including the famous Speedwell Cavern which is said to have "A bottomless pit."
- The Northumberland National Park is home to Hadrian's Wall, a World Heritage Site and was a defensive fortification built by the Roman Empire in northern England during the reign of Emperor Hadrian, between AD 122 and 128.
- The Norfolk Coast AONB (Area of Outstanding Natural Beauty) is sometimes considered Britain's smallest National Park in terms of size.
- The Lake District National Park has the highest mountain in England, Scafell Pike standing at 978 meters (3,209 feet) above sea level.
- The Cairngorms National Park in Scotland contains five of the six highest mountains in the UK. (Ben Macdui, Braeriach, Cairn Toul, Sgor Gaoith and Cairn Gorm)
- Snowdonia National Park has over 100 lakes, or "llinos" in Welsh.
- The New Forest National Park was created by William the Conqueror as a hunting area.
- Dartmoor National Park inspired Sir Arthur Conan Doyle's novel "The Hound of the Baskervilles."
- The Broads is not technically a National Park, but it has similar protection and status.
- The South Downs National Park contains the iconic chalk figure, the Long Man of Wilmington is a large hill figure of a human figure holding a staff or club, carved into the side of a hill in Wilmington, East Sussex, England.
- The Yorkshire Dales National Park inspired author James Herriot's book "All Creatures Great and Small." Which followed the adventures of a young veterinary surgeon in the Yorkshire Dales during the 1930s.
- The North York Moors National Park is famous for its heather bloom,

turning the landscape purple in late summer.
- The Pembrokeshire Coast National Park is a haven for marine life, including seals and dolphins.
- The Brecon Beacons National Park contains the highest mountain in southern Britain, Pen y Fan.
- The Peak District National Park has a rich mining history, including the Blue John Cavern, famous for its semi-precious stone "Blue John" also known as Derbyshire Spar, which is a form of fluorite exhibiting various hues of purple, blue, and yellow.
- Exmoor National Park is home to the unique Exmoor Pony, one of Britain's oldest horse breeds.
- The Northumberland National Park contains the ancient hill fort of Yeavering Bell.
- The Norfolk Coast AONB is known for its seal colonies and diverse birdlife.
- The Lake District National Park inspired Beatrix Potter's beloved children's books.
- The Cairngorms National Park is a hotspot for winter sports, including skiing and snowboarding.
- Snowdonia National Park has over 1,400 miles of public footpaths, making it a paradise for hikers.
- The New Forest National Park is home to a large population of free-roaming ponies, cattle, and pigs.
- Dartmoor National Park is famous for its ancient standing stones, known as "tors." They are granite rock formations shaped by weathering, resulting in distinct and often eerie-looking rocky outcrops scattered across the landscape
- The Broads are a popular destination for boating, with over 125 miles of navigable waterways.
- The Peak District National Park has over 65 species of breeding birds, including the iconic peregrine falcon.
- The South Downs National Park contains the iconic white chalk cliffs of the Seven Sisters.
- The Yorkshire Dales National Park is home to the famous Three Peaks

challenge, which involves climbing Pen-y-Ghent, Whernside, and Ingleborough in one day.

- The Pembrokeshire Coast National Park has been designated as a Special Area of Conservation due to its diverse wildlife and habitats.
- The Brecon Beacons National Park is renowned for its stunning waterfalls, including the famous Sgwd yr Eira.
- Exmoor National Park is one of the best places in Britain to spot red deer, the largest land mammal in the UK.

16

War Time Britain

A dark era in Britain's History, wartime took its toll on all who lived through it. I am proud to say that those who fought for Britain then have allowed us now to live the lives we live and we must never forget their sacrifices.

- During World War II, Britain was led by Prime Minister Winston Churchill, who became an iconic figure for his leadership during the war.
- The Blitz, a series of devastating German air raids on British cities, began in September 1940 and lasted until May 1941. They were aimed at weakening the morale of the British population and disrupting industry and infrastructure.
- The term "Blitz" comes from the German word "Blitzkrieg," meaning "lightning war."
- Children were evacuated from cities to the countryside during the war to protect them from bombing raids.
- The Women's Land Army was established during WWII to recruit women to work on farms and in agriculture.
- Rationing was introduced in Britain during the war to ensure fair distribution of scarce resources such as food, clothing, and fuel. People were given a "Ration Book" to keep track of their rations.
- The Ministry of Information issued posters with slogans such as "Keep Calm and Carry On" to boost morale during the war.

- The D-Day landings on June 6, 1944, marked the Allied invasion of Normandy, France, and a turning point in the war, leading to the liberation of Western Europe from Nazi occupation.
- The Battle of Britain, fought in the skies over Britain in 1940, saw the Royal Air Force (RAF) successfully repelling German attacks. The RAF and British anti-aircraft defences claimed to have shot down approximately 1,887 German aircraft, while some estimates put the number as high as 2,698.
- The Home Guard, also known as "Dad's Army," was a volunteer defence force made up of older men and those ineligible for regular military service.
- The Bletchley Park codebreakers, including Alan Turing, played a crucial role in deciphering German Enigma codes. The Enigma machine was a highly complex encryption device used by the German military during World War II to secure their secret communications, but its code was eventually cracked by British codebreakers at Bletchley Park.
- "Operation Mincemeat" involved a fake corpse carrying false information, which misdirected German attention from the real D-Day landing location.
- The "Dig for Victory" campaign encouraged people to grow their own food in gardens and allotments to supplement rationed supplies.
- Landmines were placed on beaches to prevent enemy landings, leading to the phrase "mining the beaches."
- "Make Do and Mend" was a slogan encouraging people to repair and reuse clothing and household items to save resources.
- The Anderson shelter was a small, prefabricated air-raid shelter used by families to protect themselves during bombing raids.
- Propaganda films, such as "Mrs. Miniver," were produced to boost morale and promote the war effort.
- The London Underground stations were used as air-raid shelters during the Blitz.
- The Battle of the Atlantic was a prolonged struggle to protect vital supply lines from German U-boats.
- Britain experienced rationing until 1954, nine years after the end of WWII.
- Many children received gas masks to carry with them at all times in case

of gas attacks.
- The British Merchant Navy played a crucial role in transporting goods and personnel across the Atlantic during the war.
- Coventry Cathedral was famously destroyed during a German bombing raid, and a new cathedral was built next to the ruins as a symbol of reconciliation.
- The Royal Navy's victory over the German battleship Bismarck in 1941 was a significant moment in the war.
- The "V for Victory" sign, made with the index and middle fingers raised, became a symbol of resistance.
- The "Blackout" required everyone to cover their windows at night to avoid providing landmarks for enemy bombers.
- The Wrens (Women's Royal Naval Service) and the ATS (Auxiliary Territorial Service) allowed women to serve in various military roles.
- The British "Tommy" was the nickname for a British soldier, and "Jerry" was the nickname for a German soldier.
- The "Dam Busters" raid in 1943 targeted German dams with bouncing bombs, causing significant damage.
- The Special Operations Executive (SOE) conducted sabotage and espionage operations behind enemy lines.
- The British Army used dummy tanks and other decoys to deceive the enemy about troop movements.
- The British government encouraged recycling during the war to conserve resources.
- The "Pigeon Service" used homing pigeons to carry vital messages.
- British cities, including London, suffered from widespread destruction and loss of life during the Blitz.
- The "Battle of the Barges" involved small boats evacuating British troops from Dunkirk during Operation Dynamo.
- The Battle of El Alamein in North Africa was a crucial victory for the Allies. It is estimated that there were around 13,500 Allied casualties and approximately 10,000 Axis (German and Italian) casualties during the two-month-long battle, which took place from October 23 to November

4, 1942.

- The British Navy helped evacuate Allied troops from the beaches of Dunkirk in 1940. The "Little Ships of Dunkirk" were civilian boats that participated in the evacuation.
- The "Hawker Hurricane" and the "Supermarine Spitfire" were iconic British fighter planes.
- The "Great Escape" was an attempt by Allied prisoners to break out of a German POW camp. This inspired the movie.
- "Victory Gardens" were planted in public spaces to grow vegetables for the war effort.
- The British "Home Front" was the term used to describe civilian life during the war.
- The British spirit of resilience and determination during WWII is often referred to as "the spirit of the Blitz."

17

British Politics

A new Prime Minister every week you say? This chapter gives you a run down of some facts about our good old British Politics.

- The UK Parliament is one of the oldest continuous representative assemblies in the world, with roots dating back to the 13th century.
- The Parliament of the United Kingdom consists of two houses: the House of Commons and the House of Lords.
- The Prime Minister is the head of government in the UK and is usually the leader of the political party that has the most seats in the House of Commons.
- The official residence of the Prime Minister is 10 Downing Street in London.
- The British monarch's role in politics is largely ceremonial, and they have limited powers in government.
- The House of Commons is made up of Members of Parliament (MPs) who are elected by the public in general elections.
- The House of Lords is composed of appointed members, including life peers, bishops, and hereditary peers.
- The King's Speech, delivered at the State Opening of Parliament, outlines the government's agenda for the upcoming session.
- The concept of parliamentary democracy evolved in the UK and has been adopted by many countries around the world.

- The UK's political party system is dominated by the Conservative Party and the Labour Party, but there are several other smaller parties, including the Liberal Democrats and the Scottish National Party (SNP).
- The first woman to become Prime Minister of the UK was Margaret Thatcher, who served from 1979 to 1990. Frequently termed "The Iron Lady" due to her strong and unwavering leadership style and her tough stance on political and economic issues during her time as Prime Minister of the United Kingdom.
- The Speaker of the House of Commons is responsible for maintaining order during debates and discussions.
- The UK has a constitutional monarchy, meaning the country is governed by a constitution, with the monarch as the head of state.
- The Palace of Westminster, where the UK Parliament meets, is a World Heritage Site.
- The UK has had three female Prime Ministers to date: Margaret Thatcher, Theresa May and Liz Truss.
- The longest-serving Prime Minister in UK history was Sir Robert Walpole, who held office for over 20 years from 1721 to 1742.
- The "West Lothian question" refers to the issue of Scottish MPs voting on matters affecting England, while English MPs cannot vote on similar matters affecting Scotland.
- The UK held a referendum in 2016 in which a majority voted to leave the European Union, leading to the process known as Brexit.
- The House of Lords Act 1999 significantly reduced the number of hereditary peers who could sit in the House of Lords.
- The House of Commons was originally established in the Palace of Westminster in 1265.
- The UK Parliament has the power to pass laws and legislation that apply to the whole country.
- The Parliament of the UK has the power to dissolve and call for general elections.
- The Chancellor of the Exchequer is responsible for the UK's economic and financial matters.

- The "father of the House" is the longest-serving member of the House of Commons.
- The UK Parliament's sessions are known as "Parliaments," and each Parliament typically lasts for about five years.
- The UK was the first country to introduce the concept of a secret ballot in parliamentary elections.
- The political parties in the UK are often divided into "left-wing" and "right-wing" ideologies.
- The UK Parliament meets at the Palace of Westminster in London.
- The UK was the first country to grant women the right to vote in parliamentary elections in 1918 (limited to women over 30), and in 1928, this was extended to all women over 21.
- The "Glorious Revolution" of 1688 led to the establishment of parliamentary supremacy over the monarchy.
- The UK Parliament is the supreme legal authority in the country.
- The House of Commons has 650 MPs representing different constituencies across the UK.
- The UK Parliament has the authority to scrutinize and hold the government accountable.
- The UK Parliament has the power to declare war.
- The Labour Party was founded in 1900 by trade unionists and socialist groups.
- The House of Lords Act 1999 significantly reduced the number of hereditary peers who could sit in the House of Lords.
- The State Opening of Parliament is a grand ceremonial event attended by the monarch, during which the King's Speech is delivered.
- The Parliament Act 1911 reduced the power of the House of Lords to veto legislation passed by the House of Commons.
- The first Prime Minister of the UK was Sir Robert Walpole, who is often considered the de facto first holder of the office.
- The Leader of the Opposition is the leader of the largest political party not in government.
- The UK Parliament is responsible for making and passing laws, known as

Acts of Parliament.
- The UK Parliament has the power to approve government spending and taxation.

18

Traditional British Folklore

The following chapter is all about traditional British Folklore stories, where they originate from and what they are about.

- King Arthur and the Knights of the Round Table (England): The legendary tale of a noble king and his knights who sought the Holy Grail and defended Camelot.
- Robin Hood (England): The story of a skilled archer and outlaw who stole from the rich to give to the poor in Sherwood Forest.
- Jack the Giant Killer (England): The daring adventures of a young boy who defeats ferocious giants threatening his kingdom.
- The Loch Ness Monster (Scotland): The mysterious creature is said to reside in Loch Ness, one of Scotland's largest and deepest lakes.
- The Green Man (Various): A mythical figure often depicted with foliage growing from his mouth, representing nature's connection with humanity.
- Beowulf (England): An epic poem about a heroic warrior who battles monsters to save his people.
- Tam Lin (Scotland): A tale of a young woman who rescues her lover from the clutches of the Faerie Queen on Halloween night.
- The Legend of Lady Godiva (England): The story of a noblewoman who rode through the streets of Coventry naked to protest her husband's taxes.

- The Pied Piper of Hamelin (England): The mysterious piper who lured rats away from a town, only to exact revenge by leading away the children when his payment was refused.
- The Brownie (Scotland): A helpful household spirit that performed chores in exchange for small gifts.
- The Beast of Bodmin Moor (England): A mysterious large cat-like creature said to roam the moors of Cornwall.
- The Wild Hunt (Various): A spectral procession of ghostly horsemen and hounds, led by mythical figures such as Odin or King Arthur.
- The Selkie (Scotland): A creature that can transform from a seal to a human, often depicted in romantic tales.
- The Grey Lady of Glamis Castle (Scotland): The ghostly apparition believed to haunt the historic Glamis Castle.
- The Mary Celeste (England): The mysterious tale of a ship found abandoned in the Atlantic Ocean without a crew.
- The Mermaid of Zennor (England): A mythical mermaid said to have lured a local man into the sea with her enchanting song.
- The Changeling (Various): A tale of fairies replacing a human child with one of their own.
- The Headless Horseman (England): The ghostly rider who haunts the roads at night, often associated with Sleepy Hollow.
- The Brown Man of the Muirs (Scotland): A mysterious figure said to appear on the muirs (moors) as a harbinger of bad luck.
- The Lambton Worm (England): The legend of a brave knight who slays a monstrous worm terrorizing a village.
- The Curse of Macbeth (England/Scotland): A superstition that speaking the name of "Macbeth" in a theater brings bad luck.
- The Trow (Shetland Islands): A mischievous and sometimes malevolent supernatural creature in Shetland folklore.
- The Grey Mare of Widdecombe (England): A ghostly apparition that haunts the churchyard in Widecombe-in-the-Moor, Devon.
- The Redcaps (Scotland): Malevolent fairy creatures said to live in old castles and guard ancient ruins.

- The Hobyahs (England): A tale of a family's bravery in facing off against wicked Hobyahs threatening their home.
- The Lambton Worm (England): The legend of a brave knight who slays a monstrous worm terrorizing a village.
- The Devil's Bridge (Wales): A story of a pact with the devil to build a bridge, which the devil tries to claim as his payment.
- The Grey Man of Ben MacDhui (Scotland): A giant spectre said to haunt the mountain of Ben MacDhui.
- The White Lady of Skipsea Castle (England): The ghost of a woman said to wander the ruins of Skipsea Castle.
- The Bogeyman (Various): A mythical creature used to frighten children into behaving.
- The Demon Dog of Dartmoor (England): A legendary black dog said to roam the moors of Dartmoor.
- The Demon of Spreyton (England): A story of a devilish creature that terrorized a village in Devon.
- The Gwyllion (Wales): Mischievous mountain spirits that would lead travelers astray.
- The Cauld Lad of Hylton (England): The ghostly spirit of a young servant boy who haunts Hylton Castle.
- The Nuckelavee (Scotland): A malevolent water creature that brought disease and disaster.
- The Ceffyl Dŵr (Wales): A water horse that lured travellers to ride on its back before plunging into the water to drown them.
- The Barghest (England): A supernatural black dog believed to foretell death or disaster.
- The Knucker (England): The monstrous dragon is said to have lived in a well in Lyminster, Sussex.
- The Nisse/Tomte (England/Scotland): A helpful household spirit known by different names in different regions.
- The Giant of Cerne Abbas (England): A giant chalk figure on a hillside in Dorset, the origins of which are unclear.
- The Water Leaper (Scotland): A creature said to jump out of the water to

catch unsuspecting travellers.

- The Wild Man of Orford (England): A mysterious figure is said to have been caught and imprisoned in Orford Castle.
- The Fairy Flag of Dunvegan (Scotland): A magical flag said to possess powers of protection and luck.
- The Beast of Bodmin Moor (England): A mysterious large cat-like creature said to roam the moors of Cornwall.

19

The Commonwealth

The Commonwealth is a large collection of countries that consider Britain's monarch their sovereign.

- The British Commonwealth, also known as the Commonwealth of Nations, is a voluntary association of 54 member countries, most of which are former territories of the British Empire.
- The Commonwealth was officially established in 1931 with the signing of the Statute of Westminster.
- King Charles III is the current Head of the Commonwealth, a role he has held since 2022.
- The Commonwealth's member countries are spread across six continents, making it a truly global organization.
- India was the first country to join the Commonwealth after gaining independence from British rule in 1947.
- The Commonwealth Secretariat, based in London, serves as the central organization coordinating the activities of the member countries.
- The Commonwealth countries collectively represent around one-third of the world's population.
- The Commonwealth Games, a multi-sport event held every four years, bring together athletes from member countries.
- The values of the Commonwealth are enshrined in the Commonwealth

Charter, emphasizing principles such as democracy, human rights, and sustainable development.

- The Commonwealth does not have a formal constitution, and membership is based on voluntary adherence to its principles.
- The official Commonwealth Day is celebrated on the second Monday of March each year.
- The Commonwealth has a unique structure that allows for cooperation and consultation among member countries on various issues.
- The Commonwealth Heads of Government Meeting (CHOGM) is held every two years, providing a forum for leaders to discuss global challenges and shared priorities.
- The Commonwealth has played a significant role in advancing gender equality and empowering women through initiatives like the Commonwealth Women's Forum.
- The Commonwealth promotes cultural diversity and encourages the sharing of arts and traditions among member countries.
- English is the most widely spoken language among Commonwealth countries, but a diverse range of languages are used across the organization.
- The Commonwealth Youth Programme supports young people in their personal and professional development.
- The Commonwealth Small States Centre of Excellence aims to assist small member countries in facing unique challenges.
- The Commonwealth of Learning focuses on advancing open and distance learning opportunities.
- The Commonwealth Fund for Technical Cooperation provides assistance to member countries for development projects.
- The Maldives is the smallest member country of the Commonwealth in terms of both population and land area.
- Canada is the largest member country of the Commonwealth by land area.
- Papua New Guinea is the most linguistically diverse member country, with over 800 languages spoken.
- The Commonwealth has observer members and applicants, such as Mozambique, which is currently in the process of joining.

- The Commonwealth Blue Charter aims to promote ocean conservation and sustainable development.
- The Commonwealth has been actively involved in mediating conflicts and promoting peace and reconciliation among member countries.
- The Commonwealth Foundation supports civil society organizations in promoting democracy and human rights.
- The Commonwealth has been instrumental in advocating for global action on climate change and environmental issues.
- Cyprus was the first member country to be suspended from the Commonwealth, in 1961, but was reinstated in 1962.
- The Commonwealth Ministerial Action Group monitors and addresses issues of concern in member countries regarding democracy and human rights.
- The Commonwealth has observer missions that monitor elections in member countries to ensure free and fair voting processes.
- The Commonwealth's member countries are diverse in terms of culture, religion, and political systems.
- The Commonwealth's CommonwealthConnects initiative aims to bridge the digital divide and promote digital inclusion.
- The Commonwealth Climate Finance Access Hub assists member countries in accessing climate finance resources.
- Commonwealth Day celebrations often include a speech by the Secretary-General, cultural performances, and flag-raising ceremonies.
- The Commonwealth Foundation hosts the Commonwealth Short Story Prize, celebrating and promoting talented writers from member countries.
- The Commonwealth Games Federation promotes sport for development and social change in member countries.
- The Commonwealth Scholarship and Fellowship Plan provides educational opportunities for students from member countries to study abroad.
- The Queen's Young Leaders Programme recognized exceptional young leaders across the Commonwealth for their contributions to their communities.
- The Commonwealth's member countries are geographically dispersed,

making it a network of nations with diverse interests and perspectives.

· The Commonwealth has played a significant role in supporting countries transitioning to democracy and post-conflict reconciliation.

· The Secretariat supports member countries in the implementation of the Sustainable Development Goals (SDGs).

· The Commonwealth has a powerful symbolic role in fostering international cooperation and shared values among its diverse member countries.

20

Northern Ireland

The last individual county of our United Kingdom and the smallest. This chapter focuses on the northern part of Ireland across the Irish Sea.

- Northern Ireland is located on the northeastern part of the island of Ireland and shares a border with the Republic of Ireland to the south and west.
- The capital city of Northern Ireland is Belfast, which is also the largest city in the region.
- The official flag of Northern Ireland is the Union Jack, which represents its status as part of the United Kingdom.
- The political system of Northern Ireland is a devolved government, meaning it has its own assembly and administration with powers over certain areas, such as education and healthcare.
- The population of Northern Ireland is approximately 1.8 million people.
- The official currency of Northern Ireland is the British Pound Sterling.
- Northern Ireland has a distinct dialect known as Ulster Scots, which is a variation of the Scots language.
- The Titanic, the famous ship that tragically sank on its maiden voyage in 1912, was built in Belfast.
- Game of Thrones, a popular TV series, was primarily filmed in various locations across Northern Ireland.
- Northern Ireland is known for its stunning landscapes, including the

Mourne Mountains, Glens of Antrim, and Lough Neagh, which is the largest lake in the British Isles.

· The flag of Northern Ireland, known as the Ulster Banner, features a red hand symbol representing the province's ancient origins.

· The Ulster Museum in Belfast is home to an extensive collection of art, history, and natural science exhibits.

· Northern Ireland's national football team is nicknamed the "Green and White Army."

· The Carrick-a-Rede Rope Bridge is a famous attraction that connects the mainland to a small island off the coast of County Antrim.

· The Belfast Castle is a historic landmark that offers panoramic views of the city.

· The traditional Irish sport of hurling is also played in Northern Ireland, particularly in counties with strong Gaelic games traditions.

· The Harland and Wolff shipyard in Belfast built not only the Titanic but also many other famous ships, contributing significantly to Northern Ireland's maritime heritage.

· St. Patrick's Day is celebrated enthusiastically in Northern Ireland, with parades and cultural events held across the region.

· Bushmills, located in County Antrim, is home to the world's oldest licensed whiskey distillery.

· The Belfast City Hall is an iconic building that serves as the headquarters of Belfast City Council.

· The political situation in Northern Ireland has been historically characterized by the Troubles, a period of conflict and sectarian violence that lasted from the late 1960s until the late 1990s.

· The Good Friday Agreement, signed in 1998, brought an end to most of the violence and established a framework for peace and political reconciliation.

· The Giant's Ring is a Neolithic henge located near Belfast and is one of the largest prehistoric structures in Ireland.

· Northern Ireland has a strong musical heritage, with traditional Irish folk music and Ulster Scots tunes being an essential part of its cultural identity.

- The Mourne Wall, a dry-stone wall that stretches across the Mourne Mountains, is an impressive feat of construction.
- The "Derry Girls" TV show, set in the city of Derry/Londonderry during the Troubles, gained international popularity for its humour and portrayal of life in Northern Ireland.
- The Peace Bridge in Derry/Londonderry symbolizes the ongoing efforts for peace and reconciliation in the region.
- The Linen Hall Library in Belfast is one of the oldest libraries in Northern Ireland, founded in 1788.
- The Lough Erne Resort in County Fermanagh hosted the G8 summit in 2013, where world leaders gathered to discuss global issues.
- Northern Ireland is home to many beautiful gardens, including Mount Stewart and the Botanic Gardens in Belfast.
- The Dark Hedges, an avenue of beech trees near Ballymoney, gained fame after being featured in Game of Thrones.
- The Crumlin Road Gaol in Belfast, a former prison, now operates as a tourist attraction and conference centre.
- The Ulster Folk Museum in County Down provides a glimpse into the region's rural life and traditions.
- Belfast's Grand Opera House is a stunning Victorian-era theatre renowned for its performances.
- The Ulster Aviation Society in Belfast showcases a wide array of aircraft and aviation memorabilia.
- The River Lagan, which flows through Belfast, offers opportunities for kayaking and other watersports.
- Northern Ireland has a rich literary tradition, with writers like Seamus Heaney, C.S. Lewis, and Jonathan Swift hailing from the region.
- Ulster Fry is a traditional breakfast dish in Northern Ireland, featuring fried eggs, bacon, sausages, black and white pudding, and soda bread.
- The Glens of Antrim offer beautiful hiking trails and scenic views of the coast.
- The historic town of Carrickfergus, with its medieval castle, is a popular tourist destination.

- The Peace Lines, barriers that separate certain neighbourhoods in Belfast, are a visual reminder of the region's complex history and ongoing reconciliation efforts.

21

Popular British Sports

We do love our sport. It is a large part of British entertainment. The desire to simply beat another team, and the following feeling of epic smugness afterwards.

- Cricket is believed to have originated in England, and the world's first recorded cricket match took place in Kent in 1646.
- The modern rules of football (soccer) were codified in England in 1863 when the Football Association (FA) was formed.
- Wimbledon, the oldest tennis tournament in the world, has been held in London since 1877.
- Rugby was founded in England in 1823 when William Webb Ellis picked up the ball during a soccer match and ran with it.
- The British Isles are home to many iconic golf courses, including St. Andrews in Scotland, known as the "Home of Golf."
- The Oxford-Cambridge Boat Race, held annually since 1829, is one of the oldest rowing competitions in the world.
- The London Marathon, first held in 1981, is one of the most popular marathons globally, attracting runners from around the world. British athletes won a total of 67 medals, including 27 gold medals, at the 2012 London Olympics.
- The FA Cup, founded in 1871, is the oldest football competition in the

world.
- The British and Irish Lions, a rugby union team representing the UK and Ireland, tours countries like New Zealand, Australia, and South Africa.
- The Grand National, an iconic horse race, has been held at Aintree Racecourse in Liverpool since 1839.
- The Queen's Plate, first run in 1860, is Canada's oldest thoroughbred horse race and is named after Queen Victoria.
- The British Open, also known as The Open Championship, is the oldest golf tournament in the world, first played in 1860.
- Snooker, a popular cue sport, originated in British Army officers' messes in India during the 19th century.
- The UK is home to various unique sports, including shin-kicking, cheese rolling, and worm charming.
- The Commonwealth Games, held every four years, bring together athletes from former British colonies to compete in various sports.
- The English Premier League is one of the most popular and lucrative football leagues in the world.
- The Scottish Premier League, founded in 1998, is the highest division of professional football in Scotland.
- The All England Lawn Tennis and Croquet Club, where Wimbledon is held, was originally founded in 1868 as the All England Croquet Club.
- The Oxford and Cambridge Boat Race was initially held in Henley-on-Thames before moving to the River Thames in London.
- The British Isles are home to numerous world-class rugby stadiums, such as Twickenham in London and Murrayfield in Edinburgh.
- The British Empire Games, held in 1930, were the precursor to the Commonwealth Games.
- The Isle of Man TT is one of the most dangerous and prestigious motorcycle road races in the world.
- The Boat Race between Oxford and Cambridge has been rowed annually since 1856, except during wartime.
- The oldest football club in the world is Sheffield FC, founded in 1857.
- The Epsom Derby, first run in 1780, is considered one of the most

prestigious horse races globally.

- The British Formula 1 Grand Prix has been held annually since 1950, making it one of the oldest Formula 1 races.
- The UK is home to the world's oldest horse racing event, the Kiplingcotes Derby, first held in 1519.
- The Ryder Cup, a prestigious golf tournament contested between the United States and Europe, was first held in Worcester, Massachusetts, in 1927.
- The British Isles are renowned for their love of rugby, with strong rivalries between England, Scotland, Wales, and Ireland.
- The first recorded game of badminton was played in England in the mid-19th century.
- The UK is known for its passion for horse racing, with numerous race-courses scattered across the country.
- Darts, a popular pub game, has its origins in the United Kingdom.
- The British Grand Prix has taken place at several locations, including Silverstone and Brands Hatch.
- Horse racing enthusiasts participate in the Royal Ascot, a prestigious event attended by members of the British Royal Family.
- The Six Nations Championship is an annual rugby union competition between England, Scotland, Wales, Ireland, France, and Italy.
- The Ashes is a famous cricket series played between England and Australia, dating back to 1882.
- The Henley Royal Regatta, held annually on the River Thames, is one of the world's most prestigious rowing events.

22

Notable British Scientists and Innovations

Britain has had plenty of celebrities but we also have given the world some of the most fantastic minds too.

- Sir Isaac Newton (1642-1727): His work on classical mechanics and the laws of motion laid the foundation for modern physics.
- Charles Darwin (1809-1882): His theory of evolution by natural selection revolutionized our understanding of life's diversity and origins.
- Alexander Fleming (1881-1955): Discovered penicillin, the world's first antibiotic.
- Ada Lovelace (1815-1852): An early computer programmer who worked with Charles Babbage on his analytical engine.
- Michael Faraday (1791-1867): Pioneered electromagnetic induction and made significant contributions to the understanding of electricity and magnetism.
- James Clerk Maxwell (1839-1907): Formulated the electromagnetic theory, unifying electricity and magnetism.
- Rosalind Franklin (1920-1958): Made key contributions to the discovery of the structure of DNA through X-ray crystallography.
- Stephen Hawking (1942-2018): A theoretical physicist who made ground-breaking contributions to black hole physics and cosmology.
- Francis Crick (1916-2004): Co-discovered the structure of DNA, revealing

its role in heredity.
- John Dalton (1766-1844): Proposed the atomic theory, revolutionizing our understanding of matter.
- Dorothy Hodgkin (1910-1994): Pioneered the use of X-ray crystallography to determine the structures of complex molecules, including insulin.
- Edward Jenner (1749-1823): Developed the smallpox vaccine, one of the first successful vaccines.
- Alan Turing (1912-1954): A pioneer in computer science and artificial intelligence, instrumental in breaking the German Enigma code during World War II.
- Tim Berners-Lee (1955-): Invented the World Wide Web, revolutionizing communication and information-sharing.
- Robert H. H. White (1923-2010): Invented the portable mass spectrometer, essential in various scientific disciplines.
- Jane Goodall (1934-): A renowned primatologist who conducted ground-breaking research on chimpanzees.
- Richard Feynman (1918-1988): A physicist known for his work in quantum mechanics and his role in the investigation of the Challenger Space Shuttle disaster.
- Joseph Lister (1827-1912): Pioneered antiseptic surgery, significantly reducing infections and mortality rates.
- William Harvey (1578-1657): Discovered the circulation of blood in the human body.
- James Watt (1736-1819): Improved the steam engine, catalyzing the Industrial Revolution.
- Timothy John Berners-Lee (1955-): Invented the World Wide Web, revolutionizing communication and information-sharing.
- Charles Babbage (1791-1871): Designed the analytical engine, considered the first mechanical computer.
- John Snow (1813-1858): Investigated the cause of cholera outbreaks, pioneering the field of epidemiology.
- Dorothy Mary Crowfoot Hodgkin (1910-1994): Determined the structures of important biochemical substances through X-ray crystallography,

including penicillin and vitamin B12.

- John Logie Baird (1888-1946): Developed the first working television system.
- Joseph Priestley (1733-1804): Discovered oxygen and described its role in combustion.
- Paul Dirac (1902-1984): A pioneering physicist who made significant contributions to quantum mechanics and quantum electrodynamics.
- George Stephenson (1781-1848): A pioneer of steam locomotion, building the first practical steam locomotive for railways.
- William Gilbert (1544-1603): Conducted fundamental research on magnetism and electricity.
- James Watt (1736-1819): Improved the steam engine, catalyzing the Industrial Revolution.
- Joan Clarke (1917-1996): A cryptanalyst who played a crucial role in breaking German codes during World War II.
- David Attenborough (1926-): A natural historian and broadcaster known for his documentary series on wildlife and the natural world.
- Geoffrey Wilkinson (1921-1996): A Nobel laureate for his work on transition metal chemistry.
- Charles Lyell (1797-1875): A geologist who promoted the concept of uniformitarianism, influencing the development of modern geology.
- Oliver Heaviside (1850-1925): Made significant contributions to the understanding of electromagnetic theory and electrical engineering.
- John Boyd Dunlop (1840-1921): Inventor of the pneumatic tire.
- George Cayley (1773-1857): Considered the father of aerodynamics and the pioneer of fixed-wing flight.

23

British Films

Below are some of the Greatest British Films of all time with some cool facts. As with the TV shows some are for adults so you will have to wait until you're eighteen to watch them! Why don't you ask how many of these films your parents have seen?

- Harry Potter series: Based on the beloved books by J.K. Rowling, the film franchise became a global phenomenon.
- James Bond series: One of the longest-running and most successful film franchises in history based on the popular Ian Flemming books.
- The King's Speech: This historical drama won multiple Academy Awards, including Best Picture.
- Love Actually: The romantic comedy intertwines various love stories set during the Christmas season.
- Bridget Jones's Diary: A modern-day adaptation of Jane Austen's "Pride and Prejudice" set in London.
- Trainspotting: This gritty drama follows a group of heroin addicts in Edinburgh.
- The Full Monty: A comedy-drama about a group of unemployed men who form a male striptease act.
- Notting Hill: The romantic comedy stars Julia Roberts and Hugh Grant as an unlikely couple who meet in the vibrant neighbourhood of Notting Hill,

London.
- Four Weddings and a Funeral: This charming romantic comedy follows a group of friends through four weddings and a funeral.
- The Imitation Game: The film portrays the life of mathematician Alan Turing and his team who cracked the Enigma code during World War II.
- A Clockwork Orange: This dystopian crime film, directed by Stanley Kubrick, explores themes of violence and society's control.
- Slumdog Millionaire: The heartwarming tale of a young boy from the slums of Mumbai who competes in the Indian version of "Who Wants to Be a Millionaire?"
- 28 Days Later: This post-apocalyptic horror film follows survivors in a zombie-infested London.
- The Theory of Everything: The biographical drama tells the story of physicist Stephen Hawking and his relationship with his first wife, Jane.
- Shaun of the Dead: A comedy-horror film that brilliantly blends zombie apocalypse with British humour.
- Billy Elliot: This inspiring drama tells the story of a young boy pursuing his passion for dance against all odds.
- Pride and Prejudice: Various adaptations of Jane Austen's classic novel have been made, with the 2005 version starring Keira Knightley as Elizabeth Bennet being a standout.
- Sense and Sensibility: Another Jane Austen classic, this period drama showcases the Dashwood sisters' romantic pursuits.
- The Great Escape: This World War II film depicts a group of Allied prisoners attempting a daring escape from a German POW camp.
- Lawrence of Arabia: An epic historical drama based on the life of T.E. Lawrence during World War I.
- The Bridge on the River Kwai: Another classic World War II film about British POWs forced to build a bridge for their Japanese captors.
- Chariots of Fire: This inspiring sports drama tells the story of two athletes competing in the 1924 Paris Olympics.
- This Is England: A powerful drama set in the 1980s, exploring the lives of a group of young skinheads.

- The Wind That Shakes the Barley: This historical drama depicts the Irish War of Independence and the Irish Civil War.
- Fish Tank: The drama follows a 15-year-old girl's turbulent life in a gritty British housing estate.
- The Elephant Man: Based on the life of Joseph Merrick, who suffered from severe physical deformities.
- My Fair Lady: A classic musical adaptation of George Bernard Shaw's play "Pygmalion."
- Bend It Like Beckham: A comedy-drama about a young woman pursuing her dream of playing football despite cultural expectations.
- A Fish Called Wanda: This British-American comedy-crime film stars John Cleese, Jamie Lee Curtis, and Kevin Kline.
- About Time: A heartwarming time-travel romantic comedy-drama starring Domhnall Gleeson and Rachel McAdams.
- East Is East: A comedy-drama about a Pakistani father struggling to maintain his cultural traditions in a British setting.
- Sliding Doors: The romantic comedy-drama explores two parallel universes based on whether the protagonist catches a train or not.
- The Queen: A biographical drama about Queen Elizabeth II's reaction to the death of Princess Diana.
- Lock, Stock and Two Smoking Barrels: A crime comedy film that marked the directorial debut of Guy Ritchie.
- Harry Brown: A gritty thriller starring Michael Caine as an elderly man seeking justice for his neighbourhood.
- Wallace & Gromit: The Curse of the Were-Rabbit: An animated comedy featuring the beloved characters of Wallace and Gromit.
- The Italian Job: A classic heist film set in Italy, featuring the iconic Mini Cooper car chase scenes.
- The Imitation Game: The film portrays the life of mathematician Alan Turing and his team who cracked the Enigma code during World War II.

24

British Wildlife

Our island is home to some fantastic species of wildlife. The diversity is massive. This final chapter will take a look at everything about British Wildlife.

- The UK is home to six native species of reptiles: common lizard, slowworm, grass snake, adder, smooth snake, and sand lizard.
- The red fox is the most widespread and abundant wild mammal in the UK.
- The UK is home to over 50 species of butterflies, including the beautiful peacock butterfly and the small tortoiseshell.
- The Eurasian badger is a nocturnal mammal found throughout the UK, known for its distinctive black and white striped face.
- Hedgehogs are native to the UK and are the only British mammal with spines.
- The common frog is one of the most recognizable amphibians found in gardens and ponds across the UK.
- The puffin, with its colourful beak, is one of the most iconic seabirds found on the coasts of the UK.
- The grey seal is the larger of the two seal species found in the UK, and it's often seen basking on the shores.
- The red squirrel is native to the UK but has faced declining numbers due to competition with the invasive grey squirrel.
- The Scottish wildcat is one of the rarest and most endangered species in

the UK, with fewer than 100 individuals left in the wild.
- The common starling is known for its mesmerizing murmurations, where thousands of birds fly in coordinated patterns.
- The UK is home to a wide variety of bats, with 18 species recorded, including the common pipistrelle and the noctule bat.
- The European otter is a semi-aquatic mammal found in rivers, lakes, and coastal areas throughout the UK.
- The UK's coastline is an important habitat for various seabirds, including gannets, kittiwakes, and razorbills.
- The adder is the only venomous snake native to the UK, but its bites are rarely fatal to humans.
- The European robin is a beloved bird in the UK, often associated with Christmas due to its red breast.
- The brown hare is the fastest land mammal in the UK and can reach speeds of up to 45 miles per hour.
- The UK is home to several species of deer, including red deer, roe deer, fallow deer, and sika deer.
- The harvest mouse is the smallest rodent found in the UK, known for building intricate nests in tall grasses.
- The UK is an essential habitat for various bird species during their migration, including swallows, swifts, and cuckoos.
- The European water vole is a semi-aquatic rodent known for its burrows along riverbanks and waterways.
- The white-tailed eagle, also known as the sea eagle, is the largest bird of prey in the UK.
- The UK is home to over 600 species of birds, making it a fantastic destination for birdwatching.
- The short-eared owl is a winter visitor to the UK, favouring open landscapes such as moorlands and coastal areas.
- The common dolphin and bottlenose dolphin are two species of dolphins found in the waters surrounding the UK.
- The UK's chalk cliffs, such as the White Cliffs of Dover, are nesting sites for seabirds like fulmars and guillemots.

- The hazel dormouse is a small, hibernating mammal native to the UK, known for its long periods of dormancy during winter.
- The UK is home to several species of owls, including barn owls, tawny owls, and little owls.
- The great crested newt is one of the UK's largest newt species and is protected under conservation legislation.
- The common pipistrelle bat is one of the most abundant bat species in the UK and is often seen flying at dusk.
- The grey heron is a common sight near rivers, lakes, and coastal wetlands throughout the UK.
- The UK's heathlands, such as those found in the New Forest, provide a vital habitat for reptiles and insects.
- The UK's woodlands are home to a variety of bird species, including woodpeckers, nuthatches, and treecreepers.
- The slowworm is often mistaken for a snake but is actually a legless lizard found in gardens and grasslands.
- The common toad is a nocturnal amphibian found in gardens, woodlands, and other terrestrial habitats.
- The UK's seas and oceans are home to diverse marine life, including seals, whales, dolphins, and sharks.
- The European honey bee is an essential pollinator for many plant species in the UK, including crops and wildflowers.
- The UK's coastal areas are important nesting sites for seabirds, including puffins, kittiwakes, and razorbills.
- The UK's rivers and lakes are home to a wide variety of fish species, including salmon, trout, and perch.
- The UK's grasslands are vital habitats for many insect species, including butterflies, bees, and grasshoppers.
- The UK's bumblebees, such as the buff-tailed bumblebee and the red-tailed bumblebee, are important pollinators for flowers and crops.
- The UK's woodlands are home to various mammal species, including badgers, foxes, and squirrels.
- The UK's marshes and wetlands provide essential habitats for wetland

birds like herons, egrets, and swans.

- The UK's chalk downlands, like those found in the South Downs, support a diverse range of plant and animal species.
- The UK's mountains and uplands, such as the Scottish Highlands, are home to species like red deer, golden eagles, and ptarmigans.

II

Quizzes About Britain

I have created some quizzes based on all the facts in this Book. I also added some tougher questions for good measure! How well can you do?

25

Quiz 1 - Questions

1. What is the tallest mountain in the UK?
2. Which British scientist discovered the structure of DNA?
3. What is the famous prehistoric monument located in Wiltshire, England?
4. The UK is home to how many native species of reptiles?
5. The red squirrel is native to the UK but faces competition with which invasive species?
6. What is the national flower of Scotland?
7. Which city is known as the birthplace of The Beatles?
8. Which British monarch had the longest reign in history?
9. Which famous scientist from the UK formulated the theory of evolution by natural selection?
10. Which British author wrote the "Harry Potter" series?
11. What is the capital of Scotland?
12. What is the official language of Wales?
13. In which region of the UK is the famous "Hadrian's Wall" located?
14. The UK is home to how many national parks?
15. The iconic British landmark "Big Ben" is located in which city?
16. Which British scientist is known for pioneering the theory of electromagnetism?
17. The famous author William Shakespeare was born in which town in

England?

18. What is the largest lake in the UK by volume?
19. The "Glaswegian" accent is associated with which city in Scotland?
20. What is the national flower of England?
21. Which British scientist is famous for discovering the double-helix structure of DNA alongside Francis Crick?
22. The famous British author Charles Dickens wrote which novel about a young orphan named Oliver?
23. The UK is composed of how many countries?
24. The Loch Ness Monster is said to inhabit which Scottish lake?
25. What is the national flower of Wales?

26

Quiz 1 - Answers

1. What is the tallest mountain in the UK? **Answer: Ben Nevis**
2. Which British scientist discovered the structure of DNA? **Answer: Francis Crick**
3. What is the famous prehistoric monument located in Wiltshire, England? **Answer: Stonehenge**
4. The UK is home to how many native species of reptiles? **Answer: 6**
5. The red squirrel is native to the UK but faces competition with which invasive species? **Answer: Grey squirrel**
6. What is the national flower of Scotland? **Answer: Thistle**
7. Which city is known as the birthplace of The Beatles? **Answer: Liverpool**
8. Which British monarch had the longest reign in history? **Answer: Queen Elizabeth II**
9. Which famous scientist from the UK formulated the theory of evolution by natural selection? **Answer: Charles Darwin**
10. Which British author wrote the "Harry Potter" series? **Answer: J.K. Rowling**
11. What is the capital of Scotland? **Answer: Edinburgh**
12. What is the official language of Wales? **Answer: Welsh**
13. In which region of the UK is the famous "Hadrian's Wall" located? **Answer: England**

14. The UK is home to how many national parks? **Answer: 14**
15. The iconic British landmark "Big Ben" is located in which city? **Answer: London**
16. Which British scientist is known for pioneering the theory of electromagnetism? **Answer: James Clerk Maxwell**
17. The famous author William Shakespeare was born in which town in England? **Answer: Stratford-upon-Avon**
18. What is the largest lake in the UK by volume? **Answer: Lough Neagh**
19. The "Glaswegian" accent is associated with which city in Scotland? **Answer: Glasgow**
20. What is the national flower of England? **Answer: Rose**
21. Which British scientist is famous for discovering the double-helix structure of DNA alongside Francis Crick? **Answer: James Watson**
22. The famous British author Charles Dickens wrote which novel about a young orphan named Oliver? **Answer: Oliver Twist**
23. The UK is composed of how many countries? **Answer: 4**
24. The Loch Ness Monster is said to inhabit which Scottish lake? **Answer: Loch Ness**
25. What is the national flower of Wales? **Answer: Daffodil**

27

Quiz 2 - Questions

1. In British cuisine, what are "scones" typically served with?
2. Who is the current reigning monarch of the United Kingdom?
3. What is the famous rock formation in Northern Ireland, consisting of interlocking basalt columns?
4. What does "Howay, Man" mean?
5. What is the largest city in Scotland?
6. What is the traditional Scottish dish made of sheep's liver, heart, and lungs, minced with onions and oatmeal?
7. What is the national dish of Wales, made of leeks and cheese sauce?
8. The famous British physicist Stephen Hawking is best known for his work in which area of science?
9. In which city would you find the famous Edinburgh Castle?
10. What is the traditional English drink made from fermented apples?
11. Who is the famous British naturalist and broadcaster known for his documentaries on wildlife and nature?
12. Which famous British author wrote the novel "Alice's Adventures in Wonderland"?
13. Which British band is known for hits like "Yellow Submarine" and "Hey Jude"?
14. What is the traditional Scottish musical instrument, similar to a small

bagpipe?

15. Who was the first female British Prime Minister?

16. What is the traditional English pie filled with minced meat, onions, and potatoes?

17. Which famous British monarch reigned for over six decades and was known as the "Virgin Queen"?

18. What is the famous street in London known for high-end fashion stores and as a popular shopping destination?

19. The Giant's Causeway, a unique rock formation, is located in which country of the UK?

20. What is the UK's oldest university, founded in the early 12th century?

21. In which British city would you find the famous Roman Baths?

22. Which British author wrote the "Sherlock Holmes" detective stories?

23. Which famous British scientist is known for his work on the theory of gravity?

24. The White Cliffs of Dover are located in which region of England?

25. What is the traditional Scottish musical instrument, similar to a fiddle?

28

Quiz 2 - Answers

1. In British cuisine, what are "scones" typically served with? **Answer: Clotted cream and jam**

2. Who is the current reigning monarch of the United Kingdom? **Answer: King Charles III**

3. What is the famous rock formation in Northern Ireland, consisting of interlocking basalt columns? **Answer: Giant's Causeway**

4. What does "Howay, Man" mean? **Answer: "Come on, Man" In Geordie**

5. What is the largest city in Scotland? **Answer: Glasgow**

6. What is the traditional Scottish dish made of sheep's liver, heart, and lungs, minced with onions and oatmeal? **Answer: Haggis**

7. What is the national dish of Wales, made of leeks and cheese sauce? **Answer: Welsh Rarebit**

8. The famous British physicist Stephen Hawking is best known for his work in which area of science? **Answer: Theoretical physics and cosmology**

9. In which city would you find the famous Edinburgh Castle? **Answer: Edinburgh**

10. What is the traditional English drink made from fermented apples? **Answer: Cider**

11. Who is the famous British naturalist and broadcaster known for his documentaries on wildlife and nature? **Answer: Sir David Attenborough**

12. Which famous British author wrote the novel "Alice's Adventures in Wonderland"? **Answer: Lewis Carroll**

13. Which British band is known for hits like "Yellow Submarine" and "Hey Jude"? **Answer: The Beatles**

14. What is the traditional Scottish musical instrument, similar to a small bagpipe? **Answer: Bagpipes**

15. Who was the first female British Prime Minister? **Answer: Margaret Thatcher**

16. What is the traditional English pie filled with minced meat, onions, and potatoes? **Answer: Cottage pie**

17. Which famous British monarch reigned for over six decades and was known as the "Virgin Queen"? **Answer: Queen Elizabeth I**

18. What is the famous street in London known for high-end fashion stores and as a popular shopping destination? **Answer: Oxford Street**

19. The Giant's Causeway, a unique rock formation, is located in which country of the UK? **Answer: Northern Ireland**

20. What is the UK's oldest university, founded in the early 12th century? **Answer: University of Oxford**

21. In which British city would you find the famous Roman Baths? **Answer: Bath**

22. Which British author wrote the "Sherlock Holmes" detective stories? **Answer: Sir Arthur Conan Doyle**

23. Which famous British scientist is known for his work on the theory of gravity? **Answer: Sir Isaac Newton**

24. The White Cliffs of Dover are located in which region of England? **Answer: South East England**

25. What is the traditional Scottish musical instrument, similar to a fiddle? **Answer: Violin**

29

Quiz 3 - Questions

1. What is the famous ancient site in Scotland, composed of standing stones, circles, and cairns?
2. What is the national dish of England, traditionally consisting of mashed potatoes, sausages, and onion gravy?
3. Which famous British author wrote the novel "Pride and Prejudice"?
4. In which city is the famous University of Cambridge located?
5. What is the national flower of Northern Ireland?
6. Who is the iconic British singer known for hits like "Rocket Man" and "Your Song"?
7. Which British city is known for its annual Royal Edinburgh Military Tattoo event?
8. What is the national dish of Scotland, made from minced sheep's heart, liver, and lungs mixed with oatmeal and spices?
9. Which British scientist is known for his discovery of penicillin, a groundbreaking antibiotic?
10. The UK is composed of four countries: England, Scotland, Wales, and which other?
11. In British folklore, which mythical creature is said to guard and protect the legendary treasure hidden in Cornwall?
12. What is the traditional Scottish dance usually performed at weddings and

social gatherings?

13. The UK is home to how many World Heritage Sites?

14. What is the name of the famous royal residence situated in Scotland, used as a summer retreat by the British monarch?

15. Which British author wrote the popular fantasy series "The Chronicles of Narnia"?

16. The Tower of London is famous for housing what valuable historical item?

17. Which British author wrote the "James Bond" spy novels, starting with "Casino Royale"?

18. What is the famous residence of the British Prime Minister in the countryside of Buckinghamshire?

19. In which British city is the historic York Minster, a stunning Gothic cathedral?

20. What is the traditional English dessert consisting of a sponge cake soaked in syrup and served with custard?

21. The Giant's Causeway, known for its unique hexagonal basalt columns, is located in which country of the UK?

22. Which British scientist is known for his groundbreaking theories on gravity and planetary motion?

23. What is the name of the famous street in London that connects Trafalgar Square and Buckingham Palace?

24. What is the national dish of Wales, made of meat and vegetables cooked in a pastry crust?

25. In British folklore, what are mischievous little creatures known for their love of practical jokes and trickery?

30

Quiz 3 - Answers

1. What is the famous ancient site in Scotland, composed of standing stones, circles, and cairns? **Answer: The Orkney Islands**
2. What is the national dish of England, traditionally consisting of mashed potatoes, sausages, and onion gravy? **Answer: Bangers and mash**
3. Which famous British author wrote the novel "Pride and Prejudice"? **Answer: Jane Austen**
4. In which city is the famous University of Cambridge located? **Answer: Cambridge**
5. What is the national flower of Northern Ireland? **Answer: Flax flower (Flax bloom)**
6. Who is the iconic British singer known for hits like "Rocket Man" and "Your Song"? **Answer: Elton John**
7. Which British city is known for its annual Royal Edinburgh Military Tattoo event? **Answer: Edinburgh**
8. What is the national dish of Scotland, made from minced sheep's heart, liver, and lungs mixed with oatmeal and spices? **Answer: Haggis**
9. Which British scientist is known for his discovery of penicillin, a groundbreaking antibiotic? **Answer: Sir Alexander Fleming**
10. The UK is composed of four countries: England, Scotland, Wales, and which other? **Answer: Northern Ireland**

11. In British folklore, which mythical creature is said to guard and protect the legendary treasure hidden in Cornwall? **Answer: Piskies (Pixies)**

12. What is the traditional Scottish dance usually performed at weddings and social gatherings? **Answer: Ceilidh**

13. The UK is home to how many UNESCO World Heritage Sites? **Answer: 32**

14. What is the name of the famous royal residence situated in Scotland, used as a summer retreat by the British monarch? **Answer: Balmoral Castle**

15. Which British author wrote the popular fantasy series "The Chronicles of Narnia"? **Answer: C.S. Lewis**

16. The Tower of London is famous for housing what valuable historical item? **Answer: Crown Jewels**

17. Which British author wrote the "James Bond" spy novels, starting with "Casino Royale"? **Answer: Ian Fleming**

18. What is the famous residence of the British Prime Minister in the countryside of Buckinghamshire? **Answer: Chequers**

19. In which British city is the historic York Minster, a stunning Gothic cathedral? **Answer: York**

20. What is the traditional English dessert consisting of a sponge cake soaked in syrup and served with custard? **Answer: Sticky toffee pudding**

21. The Giant's Causeway, known for its unique hexagonal basalt columns, is located in which country of the UK? **Answer: Northern Ireland**

22. Which British scientist is known for his groundbreaking theories on gravity and planetary motion? **Answer: Sir Isaac Newton**

23. What is the name of the famous street in London that connects Trafalgar Square and Buckingham Palace? **Answer: The Mall**

24. What is the national dish of Wales, made of meat and vegetables cooked in a pastry crust? **Answer: Welsh rarebit**

25. In British folklore, what are mischievous little creatures known for their love of practical jokes and trickery? **Answer: Fairies**

31

Quiz 4 - Questions

1. Which British author wrote the "Lord of the Rings" trilogy?
2. In which city is the famous Tower Bridge located?
3. What is the national emblem of Wales, a red dragon?
4. Who is the British musician known for hits like "Rocket Man" and "Candle in the Wind"?
5. Which Scottish dish consists of a sheep's stomach filled with offal, suet, and oatmeal?
6. What is the national flower of Northern Ireland, also known as the "Shamrock"?
7. Which British scientist is credited with formulating the laws of motion and universal gravitation?
8. The Giant's Causeway is a UNESCO World Heritage Site located in which country?
9. What is the national dish of Scotland, made of fish traditionally served with chips (fries)?
10. Which British author wrote the detective novels featuring Hercule Poirot?
11. The UK's Parliament consists of two houses: the House of Commons and which other?
12. What is the famous university city in England, known for its punting on the River Cam?

13. What is the traditional Scottish dish made of oatmeal soaked in water and served with cream or honey?
14. Which famous British author created the character of Mary Poppins?
15. The iconic Stone of Scone, used in the coronation of British monarchs, is also known by what other name?
16. What is the national flower of Scotland?
17. Which British scientist is known for his work on the theory of evolution by natural selection?
18. In British folklore, what is the name of the mischievous creature known for stealing and hiding household objects?
19. What is the traditional English dessert made with pastry, apples, and sugar?
20. The famous White Cliffs of Dover are located in which region of England?
21. Which British scientist is known for his work on electromagnetism and the electromagnetic induction law?
22. What is the capital city of Wales?
23. In British politics, which term refers to the process of the UK leaving the European Union?
24. Which famous British author wrote the novel "1984," a dystopian vision of the future?
25. What is the traditional Irish musical instrument, similar to a small harp?

32

Quiz 4 - Answers

1. Which British author wrote the "Lord of the Rings" trilogy? **Answer: J.R.R. Tolkien**
2. In which city is the famous Tower Bridge located? **Answer: London**
3. What is the national emblem of Wales, a red dragon? **Answer: Red dragon (Y Ddraig Goch)**
4. Who is the British musician known for hits like "Rocket Man" and "Candle in the Wind"? **Answer: Elton John**
5. Which Scottish dish consists of a sheep's stomach filled with offal, suet, and oatmeal? **Answer: Haggis**
6. What is the national flower of Northern Ireland, also known as the "Shamrock"? **Answer: Clover (Three-leaf clover)**
7. Which British scientist is credited with formulating the laws of motion and universal gravitation? **Answer: Sir Isaac Newton**
8. The Giant's Causeway is a UNESCO World Heritage Site located in which country? **Answer: Northern Ireland**
9. What is the national dish of Scotland, made of fish traditionally served with chips (fries)? **Answer: Fish and chips**
10. Which British author wrote the detective novels featuring Hercule Poirot? **Answer: Agatha Christie**
11. The UK's Parliament consists of two houses: the House of Commons and

which other? **Answer: House of Lords**

12. What is the famous university city in England, known for its punting on the River Cam? **Answer: Cambridge**

13. What is the traditional Scottish dish made of oatmeal soaked in water and served with cream or honey? **Answer: Cranachan**

14. Which famous British author created the character of Mary Poppins? **Answer: P.L. Travers**

15. The iconic Stone of Scone, used in the coronation of British monarchs, is also known by what other name? **Answer: The Stone of Destiny**

16. What is the national flower of Scotland? **Answer: Thistle**

17. Which British scientist is known for his work on the theory of evolution by natural selection? **Answer: Charles Darwin**

18. In British folklore, what is the name of the mischievous creature known for stealing and hiding household objects? **Answer: Brownie**

19. What is the traditional English dessert made with pastry, apples, and sugar? **Answer: Apple pie**

20. The famous White Cliffs of Dover are located in which region of England? **Answer: South East England**

21. Which British scientist is known for his work on electromagnetism and the electromagnetic induction law? **Answer: Michael Faraday**

22. What is the capital city of Wales? **Answer: Cardiff**

23. In British politics, which term refers to the process of the UK leaving the European Union? **Answer: Brexit**

24. Which famous British author wrote the novel "1984," a dystopian vision of the future? **Answer: George Orwell**

25. What is the traditional Irish musical instrument, similar to a small harp? **Answer: Harp**

33

Quiz 5 - Questions

1. Which famous British author wrote the novel "Alice's Adventures in Wonderland"?
2. What is the traditional Scottish musical instrument, similar to a small bagpipe?
3. In which region of the UK would you find the famous Stonehenge?
4. Which British scientist is known for his contributions to the field of optics and the invention of the catadioptric system?
5. The Lake District National Park is located in which country of the UK?
6. What is the capital city of England?
7. Which area of the UK are "Mackems" From?
8. The Tower of London is a historic castle located on the bank of which river?
9. Which famous British scientist is known for his work on the theory of electromagnetism and electromagnetic induction?
10. In British folklore, which mythical creature is said to be a horse-like water spirit that inhabits the lochs and rivers?
11. What is the national flower of England?
12. Which British author wrote the classic novel "Wuthering Heights"?
13. The Giant's Causeway is located in which country of the UK?
14. Which British city is known for its annual Edinburgh Festival Fringe, the

world's largest arts festival?

15. What is the famous street in London known for high-end fashion stores and as a popular shopping destination?

16. The traditional Scottish dish "cullen skink" is a soup made from what main ingredient?

17. Which British prime minister is known for his leadership during World War II and his inspiring speeches?

18. What is the traditional Welsh musical instrument, similar to a harp but with a simpler design?

19. Which British author wrote the series "A Song of Ice and Fire," which inspired the TV show "Game of Thrones"?

20. The River Thames flows through which city in England?

21. What is the national dish of Northern Ireland, made with soda bread and usually served with butter and jam?

22. Which British scientist is known for his discovery of the element radium and his work on radioactivity?

23. The famous university city of Oxford is located in which country of the UK?

24. What is the traditional Scottish musical instrument, similar to a flute?

25. Which iconic bridge spans the River Thames and is a symbol of London?

34

Quiz 5 - Answers

1. Which famous British author wrote the novel "Alice's Adventures in Wonderland"? **Answer: Lewis Carroll**
2. What is the traditional Scottish musical instrument, similar to a small bagpipe? **Answer: Bagpipes**
3. In which region of the UK would you find the famous Stonehenge? **Answer: England**
4. Which British scientist is known for his contributions to the field of optics and the invention of the catadioptric system? **Answer: Sir Howard Grubb**
5. The Lake District National Park is located in which country of the UK? **Answer: England**
6. What is the capital city of England? **Answer: London**
7. Which area of the UK are "Mackems" From? **Answer: Sunderland**
8. The Tower of London is a historic castle located on the bank of which river? **Answer: River Thames**
9. Which famous British scientist is known for his work on the theory of electromagnetism and electromagnetic induction? **Answer: Michael Faraday**
10. In British folklore, which mythical creature is said to be a horse-like water spirit that inhabits the lochs and rivers? **Answer: Kelpie**
11. What is the national flower of England? **Answer: Rose**

12. Which British author wrote the classic novel "Wuthering Heights"? **Answer: Emily Brontë**

13. The Giant's Causeway is located in which country of the UK? **Answer: Northern Ireland**

14. Which British city is known for its annual Edinburgh Festival Fringe, the world's largest arts festival? **Answer: Edinburgh**

15. What is the famous street in London known for high-end fashion stores and as a popular shopping destination? **Answer: Oxford Street**

16. The traditional Scottish dish "cullen skink" is a soup made from what main ingredient? **Answer: Smoked haddock**

17. Which British prime minister is known for his leadership during World War II and his inspiring speeches? **Answer: Winston Churchill**

18. What is the traditional Welsh musical instrument, similar to a harp but with a simpler design? **Answer: Celtic harp**

19. Which British author wrote the series "A Song of Ice and Fire," which inspired the TV show "Game of Thrones"? **Answer: George R.R. Martin**

20. The River Thames flows through which city in England? **Answer: London**

21. What is the national dish of Northern Ireland, made with soda bread and usually served with butter and jam? **Answer: Ulster Fry**

22. Which British scientist is known for his discovery of the element radium and his work on radioactivity? **Answer: Marie Curie**

23. The famous university city of Oxford is located in which country of the UK? **Answer: England**

24. What is the traditional Scottish musical instrument, similar to a flute? **Answer: Tin whistle**

25. Which iconic bridge spans the River Thames and is a symbol of London? **Answer: Tower Bridge**

Please Leave This Book a Review

If you have enjoyed this book, please go on to Amazon and leave the Book a review. It will only take you a few seconds but makes a MASSIVE difference to the success of the book. The more reviews this book gets the larger the chance of other people seeing it and enjoying it too. Every review I get I appreciate massively and if I were there in person I would buy you a pint. But as I'm not you will just have to accept my sincerest thanks.

Cheers mate, Ben

To leave your review simply follow this link to the book's Amazon page or log into your Amazon Account and search your order history. Find the "Write review button" as you scroll down.

https://mybook.to/1000FactsAboutBritain

You can also scan the following huge **QR code** with your mobile phone's camera which will bring you to the Amazon book page easily. Thanks Again.

Printed in Great Britain
by Amazon